D1766841

Global Reflections on COVID-19 and Urban Inequalities series

Series Editors:

Brian Doucet, University of Waterloo
Rianne van Melik, Radboud University
Pierre Filion, University of Waterloo

This timely four-volume Shorts series explores the challenges and opportunities facing cities in the wake of the COVID-19 pandemic. Offering crucial insights for reforming cities to be more resilient to future crises, this is an invaluable resource for scholars and policy makers alike.

Titles in the series:

Volume 1: Community and Society

Volume 2: Housing and Home

Volume 3: Public Space and Mobility

Volume 4: Policy and Planning

Find out more at:

https://bristoluniversitypress.co.uk/global-reflections-on-covid-19-and-urban-inequalities

EDITED BY
BRIAN DOUCET, PIERRE FILION,
AND RIANNE VAN MELIK

VOLUME 2: HOUSING AND HOME

BRISTOL
UNIVERSITY
PRESS

First published in Great Britain in 2021 by

Bristol University Press
University of Bristol
1–9 Old Park Hill
Bristol
BS2 8BB
UK
t: +44 (0)117 954 5940
e: bup-info@bristol.ac.uk

Details of international sales and distribution partners are available at
bristoluniversitypress.co.uk

© Bristol University Press 2021

British Library Cataloguing in Publication Data
A catalogue record for this book is available from the British Library

ISBN 978-1-5292-1896-1 hardcover
ISBN 978-1-5292-1897-8 ePub
ISBN 978-1-5292-1898-5 ePdf

The right of Brian Doucet, Pierre Filion, and Rianne van Melik to be identified as editors of
this work has been asserted by them in accordance with the Copyright, Designs and Patents
Act 1988.

Cover design by blu inc, Bristol
Front cover image: Iain Tall/alamy.com

Contents

List of Figures

Notes on Contributors

Dennis Archambault is the Vice President of Public Affairs and Authority Health and a Communications Chair of Senior Housing Preservation – Detroit, US.

Rachel Armitage is a Professor of Criminology at the School of Human and Health Sciences, University of Huddersfield, UK.

Zeynep Atas is an Assistant Professor and the Head of the Department of Architecture, Mardin Artuklu University, Turkey.

Yuvacan Atmaca is an Assistant Professor in the Department of Architecture, Mardin Artuklu University, Turkey.

Kamalika Banerjee is a doctoral candidate at the National University of Singapore, Singapore.

Philip Brown is a Professor of Housing and Communities at the School of Human and Health Sciences, University of Huddersfield, UK.

Federico Camerin is Postdoctoral Researcher in Urban Planning at the Università IUAV di Venezia, Italy.

Alma Clavin is an Urban Planner and Geographer working as a Postdoctoral Researcher at the School of Geography, University College Dublin, Ireland.

Samadrita Das is a PhD student at the Tata Institute of Social Sciences, Mumbai, India.

Julia de Kadt leads the Gauteng City-Region Observatory's Quality of Life survey team in South Africa.

Faryal Diwan is a Social Planning Associate at the Social Development Centre Waterloo Region, Canada.

Brian Doucet is an Associate Professor and Canada Research Chair in the School of Planning at the University of Waterloo, Canada.

Luca Maria Francesco Fabris is an Associate Professor in Environmental Design at the Politecnico di Milano, Italy.

Pierre Filion is a Professor in the School of Planning at the University of Waterloo, Canada.

Amanda Furiasse is a Professor of Religion at Hamline University, US.

Phil Hubbard is a Professor of Urban Studies at King's College London, UK.

Derek Hyra is an Associate Professor of Urban Policy at American University, US.

Carla Maria Kayanan is a Postdoctoral Researcher at the School of Geography, University College Dublin, Ireland.

Loretta Lees is a Professor of Human Geography at the University of Leicester, UK.

Liangni Sally Liu is a Senior Lecturer at Massey University, New Zealand.

James McQuaid is a Doctoral Student in the Department of History at Wayne State University, US.

Leanne Monchuk is a Senior Lecturer in Criminology at the School of Human and Health Sciences, University of Huddersfield, UK.

Niamh Moore-Cherry is an Associate Professor in the School of Geography, University College Dublin, Ireland.

Dillon Newton is a Research Associate at the School of Human and Health Sciences, University of Huddersfield, UK.

Alexandra Parker is a Senior Researcher at the Gauteng City-Region Observatory, South Africa.

Tam E. Perry is an Associate Professor at Wayne State University's School of Social Work and a Research Chair of Senior Housing Preservation – Detroit, US.

Guanyu Jason Ran is a Lecturer at Waikato Institute of Technology (Wintec), New Zealand.

Brian Robson is an Executive Director (Policy and Public Affairs) at the Northern Housing Consortium, UK.

Claudia Sanford is a Tenant Organizer at United Community Housing Coalition and a Chair of Senior Housing Preservation – Detroit, US.

Lukas Stevens is a PhD candidate at McGill University's School of Urban Planning, Canada.

Sher Afgan Tareen is a Postdoctoral Fellow at Morgan State University's Center for the Study of Religion and the City, US.

Rebecca Tunstall is a Professor Emerita of Housing Policy and a former Director of the Centre for Housing Policy at the University of York, UK.

William Turman is a graduate student at the School of Planning of the University of Waterloo, Canada.

Rianne van Melik is an Assistant Professor at the Institute for Management Research, Radboud University Nijmegen, the Netherlands.

Yu Wang is an Associate Professor at Capital Normal University, China.

Rosalie Warnock is a PhD student at the School of Geography at Queen Mary University of London, UK.

Wescley Xavier is an Associate Professor at the Federal University of Viçosa, Brazil and a Visiting Researcher at the Centre for Mobilities Research, Lancaster University, UK.

Acknowledgments

This volume is one of four in the Global Reflections on COVID-19 and Urban Inequalities series, edited by Brian Doucet, Rianne van Melik, and Pierre Filion. The editors of this series would like to thank Bristol University Press, in particular Emily Watt and Freya Trand, for their help and guidance while working with us to publish these books quickly. Thanks to Helen Flitton and Anna Paterson from Newgen Publishing UK for their detailed and timely work on copy-editing and production. We would like to thank the anonymous reviewers of our series proposal, as well as the individual manuscripts for their helpful and constructive feedback. We would especially like to thank Brayden Wilson, an MA student in Planning at the University of Waterloo, for his coordination of the administration of this project, including his frequent and thorough correspondence with over 70 contributors that helped to keep this project on schedule. Brayden's work was supported thanks to funding from Canada Research Chairs program, under award number 950-231821.

Territorial Land Acknowledgment – Brian Doucet and Pierre Filion work at the University of Waterloo and reside in the City of Kitchener, which are situated on the Haldimand Tract, land that was promised to the Haudenosaunee of the Six Nations of the Grand River, and is within the traditional territory of the Neutral, Anishinaabeg, and Haudenosaunee peoples.

Preface to All Four Volumes of Global Reflections on COVID-19 and Urban Inequalities

You are currently reading one of the four volumes of Global Reflections on COVID-19 and Urban Inequalities, which jointly explore schisms the pandemic has both revealed and widened, and measures taken to mitigate or eradicate these societal gaps. The aim of this series of edited volumes is to bring together a collection of critical urban voices across various disciplines, geographies, and perspectives in order to examine the urban challenges of COVID-19 and its impact on new and existing inequities in cities around the world.

There are two sides to the pandemic. As a highly contagious disease, given enough time and a lack of effective mitigation to restrain its spread, COVID-19 will eventually infect a large majority of the population, regardless of income or geography. This is why many public health measures are directed at entire national (or indeed global) populations. But we have also quickly learned that COVID-19 is selective in its effects – for instance, based on age and comorbidity – and that the pandemic and responses to it exacerbate fault lines traversing cities, societies, and, indeed, the world order.

There is a clear urban dimension to these inequities. Some parts of the city and some populations who reside in cities are more likely to contract and spread the virus. COVID-19 is thus an amplifier of pre-existing social divisions. Access to medical treatment and possibilities to physically isolate from potential infection are unevenly distributed. So too are the consequences of policy responses, such as lockdowns, the economic impacts of the pandemic, and the individual and political reactions it prompts. The pandemic has therefore increased divisions such as between young and old, rich and poor, left and right, and countless other societal dichotomies. As a result, experiences of urban life during the pandemic vary greatly. Where these impacts of the pandemic intersect with pre-existing racism, ageism, sexism, ableism, and spatial divisions within the city, the consequences have been particularly severe. As we write this preface, vaccines are starting to be produced, distributed, and administered. This poses new questions: will we emerge from the pandemic thanks to these vaccines? How equitable will the distribution of vaccines be within countries and at the global scale?

This context suggests myriad potential urban futures. The planning, policy, and political choices made in the short term will impact the medium- and long-term trajectories of cities and the lives of their residents. Moving forward, the challenge is how to ensure that planning and policy responses to the pandemic do not further exacerbate pre-existing inequalities and injustices that were amplified because of COVID-19. Therefore, there is a need for engaged, critical urban scholarship in order to ensure that issues of social justice and equity are front and center, not only in academic debates, but in rapidly evolving planning, policy, and public discussions that will shape these urban futures. Our four volumes suggest pathways that can help make this possible.

Rather than speculate, however, this book, and its three companions in our series, unites well-informed, reflective, and empirically grounded research from around the world to contextualize the new and amplified inequities brought about by COVID-19. The divisions that are apparent during the pandemic are not treated in isolation; they are firmly situated as part of long-term trends and broader narratives about cities, places, communities, and spaces.

Critical urban research during the pandemic

The first accounts of the novel coronavirus that would become known as COVID-19 emerged late in 2019 in Wuhan, China. Over the first months of 2020, the virus spread around the world. On March 11, 2020, the World Health Organization declared a global pandemic. Schools and businesses closed, office workers were told to work from home, and public spaces were shut. International travel came to a virtual stand-still. Varying degrees of lockdown restricted the movements of people outside of their homes. In public, keeping distance from others and wearing facemasks became the norm. While the exact timing of these measures varied by country, by the summer of 2020, the majority of the world's population had experienced most of them. While the lockdowns did 'flatten the contagion curve', as restrictions of movement and activities were lifted, after a period of relative stability, infection rates took off again in the fall of 2020 and into 2021, reaching levels much higher than those experienced during the first wave.

As academics, we transitioned our own work during this time by setting up home offices, switching our teaching to online platforms and adapting our research methodologies. The specifics of our own research shifted as it became impossible to study contemporary cities without assessing the impact of COVID-19. The more we examined our own research, however, it became apparent that the key questions and approaches driving our work remained central to interpreting this new reality. The inequities we were already examining in housing, transportation, public space, metropolitan regions, and planning systems took on new dimensions because of the pandemic. But most of the inequalities that are so central and visible during the pandemic were themselves not new; they were building, in different ways, on the pre-existing inequalities of cities before COVID-19. It soon became clear that COVID-19 was exacerbating and amplifying existing socio-economic and spatial inequities, even more than it was creating entirely new ones.

The pace of change during the pandemic poses a particular dilemma for researchers, who usually benefit from sufficient time to reflect and analyze. On the one hand, jumping too quickly to conclusions leads one to speculate rather than reflect, 'opinionate' rather than research. Academics are not journalists and it is not our task to provide real-time accounts and assessment of change.

On the other hand, as critical urban scholars, we must contribute to the discussions about the myriad ways COVID-19 is reshaping urban spaces and the lives of their inhabitants. Critical voices are more important now than ever, especially since cities face such uncertain futures and the responses to the pandemic will shape cities and urban life for years to come. COVID-19 has created urban challenges unprecedented in our lifetime. The pandemic has torn back the curtain on uneven social, spatial, and racial processes of urbanization that were previously downplayed in mainstream planning and policy debates. They have rendered visible some of what was previously invisible.

This context also gives rise to new possibilities and ideas that were once at the fringes of urban debates, such as closing streets to cars, which have been put into practice in cities around the world. But again, critical scholarship and research is necessary in order to study to what extent these planning and policy responses to the pandemic play a role in impacting (and potentially augmenting) the inequalities and injustices that are central to cities in the 21st century.

In short, it is simply not possible for urban researchers to 'sit this one out' while the dust settles. While academics may prefer to conduct research after the fact, this may be years into the future and after many important decisions have long been made. The challenge is therefore to strike a delicate balance between a slower, contemplative, and reflective approach to scholarship, while still striving to influence broader, rapidly evolving debates. We believe that our approach to this edited series strikes the right tone between these two important approaches.

The development of this edited series

Specifically, this four-part collection emerged from a meeting between our editorial team – Brian Doucet, Rianne van Melik, and Pierre Filion – and Bristol University Press in April 2020, wherein we were asked to assemble a rapid response book dealing with cities and the COVID-19 pandemic. As an editorial team, our approach has been to balance the need to make active contributions to rapidly shifting debates, while also reflecting on the impact the pandemic was having on urban inequities. We decided that short chapters, highly accessible to a diverse audience of scholars, students, professionals, planners, and an informed public, would be most suitable. The short nature of these chapters means that they fall somewhere between a typical media piece and a full-length peer-reviewed article.

A broad call for chapters was launched in mid-June 2020. Throughout various listservs and on social media, we invited researchers to reflect on how COVID-19 has impacted new and existing inequalities in cities throughout the world. We welcomed chapters that dealt with any urban topic and featured perspectives and voices not always central to mainstream scholarly, planning, or policy debates, including some co-written by non-academic authors.

The response to our invitation was overwhelming. We received many more abstracts than containable in a single volume. After a rigorous evaluation of the abstracts, we invited selected researchers to write full chapters. Keeping the best of these chapters we found ourselves with a sufficient number of chapters for four volumes. The volumes were organized around the four main themes dominating the submitted chapters.

Given the edited nature of the book, the global scale of its chapters and the wide scope of its object of study, there are inevitable gaps in the coverage of events relating to the pandemic, the reactions it has prompted, and the impact of all of this on different social groups. Also, it has proven impossible to provide cases from all parts of the world. All the same, the volumes do offer broad perspectives on different aspects of COVID-19 and their manifestation in different countries and continents. One of our goals was to include scholars from a variety of career phases, including early career researchers and graduate students, and to welcome chapters written in partnership with non-academic colleagues, many of whom offer insightful perspectives of lived experiences during the pandemic.

Each of the four volumes deals with a separate theme: Volume 1 is centered on Community and Society; Volume 2 deals with Housing and Home; Volume 3 examines Public Space and Mobility; and Volume 4 focuses on Policy and Planning. Each volume can be read as a stand-alone book, with a coherent theme, structure, introduction, and conclusion. But when read together, these four volumes synthesize research that reflects on the different ways in which the COVID-19 pandemic is reshaping urban inequities. While we have divided the volumes thematically, it is becoming increasingly clear that issues of housing, land use, mobility, urban design, and economic development (issues long siloed in urban debates) all need to be part of the same conversation about contemporary and future urban challenges. This is particularly true if social justice, equity, and the right to the city are to be central to the conversation. Many chapters throughout the series therefore focus on how COVID-19 *intersects* with different forms of inequality and injustice.

The timing for this project is particularly important. We gave contributors the summer of 2020 to write their chapters. Chapters were put together, not in the heated uncertainty of those first few months, but rather during a period when initial reflection on the pandemic's first wave became possible. While some chapters rely on media reports or carefully reflect on the early days of COVID-19, others draw on important and insightful fieldwork carried out during the spring and summer of 2020.

Much will have changed between when the volumes were written and when the series is available on physical and virtual bookshelves. This edited series is not a journalistic account of the pandemic. Instead, these volumes are a collective account of the first months of the pandemic, assembled with the idea that the knowledge, voices, and perspectives found within these volumes are necessary to shaping responses to the pandemic. The chapters presented in these four volumes serve as essential documentation and analysis of how the pandemic initially manifested itself within cities around the world, cities that were already becoming more economically, socially, racially, and spatially unequal. Understanding the early phases of this global pandemic is essential to dealing with its next waves and planning for the post-pandemic period. Likewise, understanding the consequences of how the pandemic intersects with urban inequalities is necessary in order to create more equitable and socially just cities.

ONE

Introduction

Brian Doucet, Pierre Filion, and Rianne van Melik

"We're all in this together" was one of the first rallying cries of the pandemic. It could be heard (and still can be heard) from politicians and businesses. In March 2020, it was also a key message from the World Health Organization (WHO, 2020). However, critical scholarship quickly dismissed this message as it did not reflect what was happening on the ground. As discussed in Volume 1, it is abundantly clear that the COVID-19 pandemic was not a great 'equalizer', but rather an event whose impact intersected with a myriad of pre-existing inequalities affecting different people, places, and geographic scales.

While the virus itself does not discriminate between rich and poor, Black and White, apartment or house, its impact has been highly uneven as it finds weak spots in society, amplifying pre-existing inequalities and creating new ones. In many instances, these pre-existing inequalities were amplified by the continued financialization and commodification of housing (Marcuse and Madden, 2016; August and Walks, 2018), and more than a decade of austerity imposed after the 2008–09 financial crisis. Nowhere is this more apparent than in housing. Cuts to housing that disproportionately affected those on low incomes, women, racialized populations, and persons with disabilities were some of the major austerity measures in cities and countries around the world (Vilenica et al, 2020).

Despite these cuts and neoliberal approaches to planning and policy before the pandemic, housing has become a central pillar of governmental and public health approaches to fighting the virus. Housing is key to understanding how the virus spreads. 'Staying at home' has been one of the main public health messages and central to one's ability to self-isolate and quarantine (Ren, 2020; Rogers and Power, 2020). However, for many, the home is not a place of safety. For those who lack safe, secure housing, particularly unsheltered, or homeless people, being without a house can both increase exposure to COVID-19, and create barriers in accessing health care and support (Rogers and Power, 2020; Tsai and Wilson, 2020). This is why one of the key housing responses to the pandemic has been to provide temporary shelter to these populations (Parsell et al, 2020). Instances of domestic violence have risen during the pandemic, and for many people, including LGBTQ young people, homes can be unwelcome, or unsafe spaces (Rogers and Power, 2020; Salerno et al, 2020; Vilenica et al, 2020).

Overcrowding has also been a major focus of attention, although there have been few instances of planning and policy measures to deal with it (van der Merwe and Doucet, 2021; Grant, 2020; Moos et al, 2020). Overcrowding occurs when people live in tight quarters designed for fewer inhabitants than currently reside there. Density (the number of people residing in a square kilometer) and overcrowding can be related, but they are not the same thing and there are many instances of overcrowding in communities that are not particularly dense. Density can play a role in making life during the pandemic more challenging, as Phil Hubbard (Chapter Four) describes with regard to micro-apartments in hyper-dense city centers. However, there is little evidence to suggest that population density, in and of itself, is a major contributor to spreading COVID-19 (Boterman, 2020; Hamidi et al, 2020; Moos et al, 2020). Instead, the conditions where the virus can thrive are what the Toronto-based author and placemaker Jay Pitter (2020) refers to as 'forgotten densities'. In these economic, social, and spatially peripheral areas (Keil et al, 2020), overcrowded, or otherwise substandard housing conditions intersect with inadequate transportation, chronic unemployment, racism, and over-policing. These 'forgotten densities' can be found in the *favelas* of Brazil (Chapter Seven), peripheral estates in Dublin (Chapter Seventeen) or rooming houses in Kitchener (Chapter Sixteen).

While housing is central to these stories, these conditions intersect with issues of land use, racism, transportation, economic development, and inequality. This is why our volume on housing and inequality is less focused on bricks and mortar questions and more centered on how identities such as class, race, gender, ability, and age all intersect with housing to create uneven experiences and outcomes during the pandemic (see also Volume 1).[1] It has been demonstrated, for example, that those in the lowest income groups and households coming from minority, racialized backgrounds are most-likely to reside in overcrowded housing (Hall et al, 2020; McKee et al, 2020; Patel et al, 2020).

Because of this, home has been central to our variegated experiences of the pandemic and, despite the uniform messaging of the 'stay at home' guidelines, life during lockdown was neither uniform nor equal (Munro, 2020). The experiences of housing and 'home' during the first wave of the pandemic therefore offer key insights into the uneven social, spatial, and racial impacts of the pandemic. Alexis Corbière, a French MP from Saint-Denis, a poor *banlieue* outside Paris stated succinctly: 'We are locked down in our inequality' (see Willsher and Harrap, 2020). Furthermore, if we understand that for many marginalized groups, activities normally performed inside one's home are often done in public, semi-public, or semi-private spaces, the past year has also seen increased security, surveillance, and restrictions (Furiasse and Tareen,

Chapter Fourteen; Turman et al, Chapter Sixteen; see also Volume 3).

In extreme cases, the home has been a place of death. Analysis by Martine August, using data compiled by Nora Loretto showed that in some long-term care homes in Canada, more than 40 percent of residents died because of COVID-19, trends which were worse in private, for-profit facilities, rather than in public ones (August, 2020). Lukas Stevens (Chapter Eight) provides more insight into this by focusing on the precarious working and living conditions of employees at long-term care facilities. But even in less extreme instances, the concept of home – both the physical dwelling and the private spaces associated with one's home – are anything but secure, and the experience of the pandemic has been one of fear, insecurity, and deteriorating physical and mental health. This combination of factors has led Rebecca Tunstall (Chapter Two) to describe COVID-19 as a housing disease.

It is clear that the pandemic has increased social, spatial, and economic inequalities. For critical researchers, policy makers, advocates, and civic leaders, the question now facing us is how can housing play a role in reducing, rather than exacerbating these inequalities? The challenge is how to ensure the planning, political, and policy responses to the pandemic do not work to further amplify these inequalities. These are the central issues addressed in this volume.

As Rogers and Power (2020) note, some housing policy has evolved extremely rapidly since the onset of the pandemic, while in other instances, it has remained static. There is a danger that responses to the pandemic will end up focusing on the new challenges facing many middle-class households (such as more space requirements to work from home), at the expense of the urgent needs of marginalized communities that long predate this pandemic. Vilenica et al (2020) ask the important question of who and what are the emergency measures enacted thus far actually protecting? Is it vulnerable residents and communities? Or is it dominant racial and class interests? Parsell et al (2020) look critically at temporary measures to address homelessness in Australia. Temporary is the key word. Measures such as providing emergency accommodation to unsheltered populations do not address the structural causes of homelessness. Rather than doing this out of concern for the health and well-being of homeless populations, these measures are framed from the perspective of a public health emergency where unsheltered populations are seen as a threat to the health of the wider population.

Because of the impact of COVID-19, Buckle (2021) argues that housing researchers and scholars should consider themselves to be conducting 'disaster research'. Research into recent natural disasters offer insights into how 'shock doctrines' produce policies that increase inequalities through the privatization of public assets, austerity measures, increased surveillance, and other measures (Klein, 2007). Like Parsell et al (2020), Vilenica et al (2020) suggest that the central policy goal in these cases is to preserve the status quo through temporary policies that do not address the structural conditions that produce unequal cities. Hyra and Lees (Chapter Three) posit that the foundations for the next wave of gentrification are being laid during this pandemic, citing past experiences of Hurricane Katrina and the Great Recession of 2007–09 as examples of 'disaster capitalism' that fuel further commodification of housing and gentrification. Although as Mendes (2020) notes, the last financial crisis also created the framework for networks of social movements to develop that would actively resist and challenge these further waves of gentrification. Their actions exerted pressure on governments to create rapid, if temporary responses to immediate challenges of the pandemic that 'anchor[ed] the urban struggle in housing as a human right, essential to life' (Mendes, 2020: 327).

As Rogers and Power (2020) have noted, the pandemic has brought about rapid policy change. Previously unprecedented or unthinkable housing measures have been implemented in cities and countries around the world to deal with both the health and economic impacts of the pandemic. These include temporary mortgage relief, bans on evictions, using empty hotels as shelters, and allowing encampments to remain in place. Many neighborhoods have also seen measures to improve quality of life through limiting spaces for cars and creating new public spaces (Camerin and Fabris, Chapter Six; see also Volume 3). Yet very few of these initiatives have addressed structural issues of housing that have contributed to divided cities for decades and most are designed to be temporary. Rent payments have not been cancelled, just deferred; some banks even charged interest during mortgage holidays (see Tunstall, Chapter Two). Therefore, what we have seen thus far can be interpreted as attempts to maintain the status quo of 'the exchange value of housing to be a pivotal axis of capitalist circulations' (Vilenica et al, 2020: 12) in the face of unprecedented challenges to both individual human health, households, *and* to a capitalist system that derives wealth through commodifying the basic human need for shelter (housing markets would collapse if large sections of the population could no longer afford to pay their mortgages or rents).

Housing in the age of COVID-19 is therefore an extension and amplification of a pre-existing crisis. Because of this, we take the starting point that much of what is needed does not require new solutions. As Buckle (2021), Maalsen et al (2020), Rowley et al (2020), van der Merwe and Doucet (2021), and others note, investments in new social housing and emergency shelters, banning unjust evictions, curbing property speculation, and permanent rent controls are solutions that have been called for by critical housing scholars for many years. And Roman-Alcalá (2020) reminds us, the groups that have suffered the most because of the pandemic – low-income, racialized, and marginalized communities – also struggle to find safe, secure, and affordable housing under capitalism.

Returning to the challenge of how to create more equitable housing in the wake of the COVID-19 pandemic, the chapters assembled in this volume provide key insights and perspectives. They do this by reflecting on how what is happening during the pandemic (particularly in its early phases) is connected to longer-term trends and trajectories. Included within them are important voices and knowledge that rarely feature prominently in mainstream planning, policy, and political debates. As discussed in Volume 1, vulnerable and marginalized communities rarely play a leading role in shaping responses to crises. This makes the challenge of creating a more equitable city more difficult because those who are most impacted by policy and planning are largely absent from the decision-making that profoundly shapes their lives. With that in mind, chapters in this volume draw on the experiences and knowledge of marginalized people and communities in order to amplify these perspectives within wider planning and policy debates. This is necessary in order to create equitable responses to the pandemic that address the root causes of housing challenges. This volume, and the other three in this series, attempt to amplify these perspectives to shift debates about how to respond to the pandemic, and, ultimately, shift power-relations about who decides how to address this current crisis, and move forward from it. Centering these perspectives within planning and policy debates is necessary if we are to move beyond Band-Aid solutions and progress towards creating more equitable cities.

Outline of this book

The book is divided into two parts. The first part looks at housing systems more broadly, including inter-related processes of design, finance, and policy. The section starts with Rebecca Tunstall's (Chapter Two) examination of whether COVID-19 is a housing disease. She points towards poor housing conditions, specifically overcrowding and its relationship with poor health, as being key to understanding the ongoing harms caused by the pandemic, as well as factors that inhibit abilities to contain it. With much of the population staying at home during lockdowns, issues such as a shortage of space, not enough bedrooms, and poor-quality housing take on greater importance, particularly for mental health. In addition to this, as her chapter explains, COVID-19 is a disease which exposes vulnerabilities in the UK housing system, in both the public sector and the private-market.

Derek Hyra and Loretta Lees (Chapter Three) explore two possible futures of gentrification in the post-COVID-19 city: de-gentrification, which suggests that the forces driving gentrification will cause the process to reverse, and disaster gentrification, where capital exploits the situation caused by the pandemic and gentrification continues, or even grows. As noted earlier, they argue that the health and financial disasters of the COVID-19 pandemic create new opportunities for capitalism to exploit the situation, likely producing new rounds of disaster gentrification in the years ahead.

In Chapter Four, Phil Hubbard takes a critical look at the tremendous growth in 'micro-apartments' in London and other global cities over the past decade. These small flats are not suited to a prolonged period of working from home, or the need to self-isolate. While this density has been seen as an antidote to unsustainable suburban sprawl, Hubbard argues the response to build hyper-dense developments of micro-apartments in city centers can be equally damaging for health and well-being in the age of COVID-19, and the chapter explores these challenges with respect to the inter-related concepts of privacy and intimacy. He notes that these developments fit squarely with government policies, yet actually cost far more per square meter than larger-sized units. Like Tunstall, he notes that COVID-19 has exposed a housing system in the UK that was essentially broken; Hubbard suggests that privacy should be a priority for post-COVID-19 housing policy, especially in dense developments.

The role of design is further explored by Zeynep Atas and Yuvacan Atmaca in Chapter Five. They examine the degree to which two very different parts of Mardin, Turkey, are able to deal with the consequences of the pandemic and provide a 'tolerant' living environment for their inhabitants. The modern, centrally planned parts of the city (which had long been favored by middle- and upper-class households) were less able to provide the basic necessities of life, and were less conducive to self-sufficiency than the old city, which grew organically over centuries and feature an economic context where mutual aid, connection to the local, and solidarity are defining characteristics. Urban design, health, and housing systems are also explored in Federico Camerin and Luca Fabris's Chapter Six on the 'Superblock' concept in Barcelona. The Superblock groups nine blocks of the city's 19th-century Eixample (Extension) neighborhoods into a tight-knit community with shared facilities that can be resilient against threats of climate change, social vulnerability, and, in today's context, the COVID-19 pandemic. Central to a Superblock is a reallocation of road space as parks, public facilities, and community spaces. This has led to a sharp decline in traffic within Superblocks, and an increase in air quality, something that is important to mitigating the spread, and effects of COVID-19.

Wescley Xavier's intersectional Chapter Seven examines how the social conditions of Black and/or poor populations in Brazilian cities has resulted in both economic and health consequences being far harsher for these groups in one of the world's most unequal countries. Housing plays a major role in this, because low-income residents can often only find housing in *favelas* on the periphery. These neighborhoods are not only far away from jobs, but also have been largely abandoned by the state and consist of substandard and overcrowded housing. This section concludes with Chapter Eight by Lukas Stevens that examines how home and work intersect at long-term care facilities in Montreal, spaces that function as both places of residence and employment. Like Xavier, Stevens highlights the relationship between poor housing conditions and precarious employment. Many workers at long-term care facilities in and around Montreal have few housing options and therefore tend to live far from the facilities they work in, and Stevens notes the ways in which the virus moves between facilities scattered throughout the region and the low-income neighborhoods where many care workers reside. He also articulates that residents of these care homes constituted 70 percent of Quebec's COVID-19-related deaths during the first wave of the pandemic.

The second part of this volume explores the experiences of housing during the COVID-19 pandemic. This includes not only stories of life during lockdown, but how the pandemic has reshaped many experiences of the home, both in terms of one's private dwelling but also other public-, semi-public- and private-spaces that perform functions associated with the 'home'.

This section begins, fittingly, with an examination of life in the first city to experience lockdown, Wuhan, China. Liangni Sally Liu, Guanyu Jason Ran, and Yu Wang (Chapter Nine) analyze the diaries of the writer Fang Fang, which provided the first account of life under lockdown and were a vital source of information about the pandemic for many Chinese citizens. However, after the diaries were published in English, public sentiment turned against Fang Fang, though her accounts remain one of the most vivid of the early phases of the pandemic.

Philip Brown, Rachel Armitage, Leanne Monchuk, Dillon Newton, and Brian Robson (Chapter Ten) outline in broad terms how housing inequalities have been exacerbated by the pandemic. Drawing on interviews with households living in poor-quality housing, they investigate how pre-existing housing conditions amplify residents' experiences of that housing. Their chapter focuses on physical characteristics of dwellings (that is, damp and heating problems) as well as social aspects (including dealing with landlords and not enough space). Poor-quality housing amplifies stress and mental health challenges in large part because people are spending most of their time at home and therefore these substandard conditions were ever-present in their lives. In Chapter Eleven, Alexandra Parker and Julia de Kadt examine the lives of elderly residents in the Gauteng city-region in South Africa, where the HIV/ AIDS pandemic has already placed a disproportionate financial and caregiving burden on the elderly. They use data from the Gauteng City-Region Observatory's Quality of Life Survey to better understand the challenges for the elderly during the COVID-19 pandemic. They find that while they may be able to absorb some of the socio-economic shocks of the pandemic better than younger generations, they are particularly vulnerable in terms of their physical and mental health.

The next two chapters explore the housing experiences during the pandemic of specific populations. Rosalie Warnock's chapter (Chapter Twelve) focuses on life under lockdown for families who have children with autism. As her research points out, it is not the challenges of autism per se that contribute to different experiences during the pandemic, but rather the pre-existing social, spatial, and economic inequalities that often manifest themselves through the home and housing. Her chapter focuses on issues of space (crowding), safety, and care, and she recommends the appropriate allocation of social housing for families who have disabled children, combined with adequate financial and practical support for adults and young carers.

Detroit was one of the first American cities where the virus arrived. In Chapter Thirteen, Tam E. Perry, James McQuaid, Claudia Sanford, and Dennis Archambault, all members of the Senior Housing Preservation – Detroit (SHP-D) coalition, discuss the ways in which the pandemic has impacted seniors in the city and chronicles the ways in which SHP-D and other organizations worked with residents to provide essential services for their community.

For many, the 'home' extends beyond a house or apartment to include schools, shops, and places of worship. In their chapter (Chapter Fourteen) on ethnic enclaves in New York and Chicago, Amanda Furiasse and Sher Afgan Tareen use this broader concept of 'home' to examine how ethnic and religious enclaves have been subject to increased police enforcement of social distancing violations within these spaces. They argue that this has been aided by smartphone apps and social media which have allowed users to report violations within spaces that were once deemed private. Kamalika Banerjee and Samadrita Das also take the idea of housing outside the realm of private dwellings and in Chapter Fifteen explore the migration of tens of thousands of laborers out of India's largest and wealthiest cities during the early days of lockdown. They walked, sometimes thousands of kilometers, back to their home villages because lockdown meant that their ability to earn livelihoods in the city had abruptly come to a halt. Their precarity was exacerbated by the withdrawal of the state in providing assistance to these laborers, generating liminal spaces of dwelling, governance, and citizenship. Already in precarious positions, Banerjee and Das argue that the pandemic generated new forms of dispossession and vulnerability for migrant laborers. As they moved from their homes to their native villages, they inhabited a state of both social and spatial liminality.

In Chapter Sixteen, William Turman, Brian Doucet, and Faryal Diwan examine the lived experiences of very low-income and marginalized residents in a mid-sized Canadian city. Their research demonstrates that the concept of 'home' often exists outside of one's own dwelling, particularly for unsheltered people. During the pandemic, many spaces that functioned as 'living rooms' closed, meaning that residents faced not only the pre-existing threats of gentrification and displacement, but a significant disruption to their daily lives due to COVID-19 as well. In a similar vein, Carla Maria Kayanan, Niamh Moore-Cherry, and Alma Clavin's chapter on inner city Dublin (Chapter Seventeen) remind us that experiences of lockdown are contextually dependent, and rely on a normative interpretation of the home as a safe, comfortable space. They write that 'already-disadvantaged communities were dispropor-tionately impacted, compounding their vulnerabilities'. Like

Turman et al, they also highlight the ways in which closing third spaces such as community centers negatively impacts low-income residents. Another trend visible in Dublin and in other case studies such as Mardin, Turkey, was that when lockdown created a void in community and public services, local community bonds became critical to resilience (see also Auerbach et al, Volume 1). Finally, a short conclusion (Chapter Eighteen) reflects on how addressing the structural inequalities rendered visible during the pandemic requires centering the lived experiences of poverty, housing precarity, and discrimination within planning and policymaking. This is necessary in order to shape a more equitable and socially-just urban future.

Note

[1] For more on intersectionality, see Crenshaw, 1991.

References

August, M. (2020) 'The coronavirus exposes the perils of profit in seniors' housing'. *The Conversation*, July 26.

August, M. and Walks, A. (2018) 'Gentrification, suburban decline, and the financialization of multi-family rental housing: the case of Toronto'. *Geoforum*, 89: 124–36.

Boterman, W. (2020) 'Urban-rural polarisation in times of the corona outbreak? The early demographic and geographic patterns of the SARS-CoV-2 epidemic in the Netherlands'. *Tijdschrift voor economische en sociale geografie*, 111(3): 513–29.

Buckle, C. (2021) 'Research during the COVID-19 pandemic: ethics, gender and precarious work'. *International Journal of Housing Policy*, 1–15, https://doi.org/10.1080/19491247.2020.1857907

Crenshaw, K. (1991) 'Mapping the margins: intersectionality, identity politics, and violence against women of color'. *Stanford Law Review*, 43(6): 1241–99.

Grant, K. (2020) 'Data show poverty, overcrowded housing connected to COVID-19 rates among racial minorities in Toronto'. *The Globe and Mail*, July 2.

Hall, K.H., Doolan-Noble, F., McKinlay, E., Currie, O., Gray, B., Gray, L., Richard, L., Stubbe, M. and Jaye, C. (2020) 'Ethics and equity in the time of Coronavirus'. *Journal of Primary Health Care*, 12(2): 102–6.

Hamidi, S., Sabouri, S. and Ewing, R. (2020) 'Does density aggravate the COVID-19 pandemic?' *Journal of the American Planning Association*, 86(4): 495–509, https://doi.org/10.1080/01944363.2020.1777891

Keil, R., Connolly, C.S. and Ali, H. (2020) 'Outbreaks like coronavirus start in and spread from the edges of cities'. *The Conversation*, February 17.

Klein, N. (2007) *The Shock Doctrine: The Rise of Disaster Capitalism*. New York: Knopf.

Maalsen, S., Rogers, D. and Ross, L.P. (2020) 'Rent and crisis: old housing problems require a new state of exception in Australia'. *Dialogues in Human Geography*, 10(2): 225–9.

Marcuse, P. and Madden, D. (2016) *In Defense of Housing: The Politics of Crisis*. New York: Verso Books.

McKee, K., Pearce, A. and Leahy, S. (2020) 'The unequal impact of COVID-19 on black, Asian, minority ethnic and refugee communities'. *UK Collaborative Centre for Housing Research*, May 6, https://housingevidence.ac.uk/the-unequal-impact-of-COVID-19-on-black-asian-minority-ethnic-and-refugee-communities/

Mendes, L. (2020) 'How can we quarantine without a home? Responses of activism and urban social movements in times of COVID-19 pandemic crisis in Lisbon'. *Tijdschrift voor Economische en Sociale Geografie*, 111(3): 318–32.

Moos, M., McCulley, A. and Vinodrai, T. (2020) *COVID-19 and urban density: evaluating the arguments*. Discussion report for the Region of Waterloo.

Munro, M. (2020) 'Life under lockdown: our complex and varied relationship with "home"'. *UK Collaborative Centre for Housing Research*, April 9, https://housingevidence.ac.uk/life-under-lockdown-our-complex-and-varied-relationship-with-home/

Parsell, C., Clarke, A. and Kuskoff, E. (2020) 'Understanding responses to homelessness during COVID-19: an examination of Australia'. *Housing Studies*, 1–14, https://doi.org/10.1080/02673037.2020.1829564

Patel, J.A., Nielsen, F.B.H., Badiani, A.A., Assi, S., Unadkat, V.A., Patel, B., Ravindrane, R. and Wardle, H. (2020) 'Poverty, inequality and COVID-19: the forgotten vulnerable'. *Public Health*, 183: 110–11.

Pitter, J. (2020) 'Urban density: confronting the distance between desire and disparity'. *Azure Magazine*, April 17.

Ren, X. (2020) 'The quarantine of a megacity: China's struggle over the coronavirus epidemic'. *International Journal of Urban and Regional Research*, www.ijurr.org/the-urban-now/the-quarantine-of-a-megacity/

Rogers, D. and Power, E. (2020) 'Housing policy and the COVID-19 pandemic: the importance of housing research during this health emergency'. *International Journal of Housing Policy*, 20(2): 177–83.

Roman-Alcalá, A. (2020) 'Thoughts on the origins, present, and future of the coronavirus crisis: marginalization, food and housing, and grassroots strategies'. *Agriculture and Human Values*, 37: 647–8.

Rowley, S., Crowe, A., Gilbert, C., Kruger, M., Leishman, C. and Zuo, J. (2020) *Responding to the pandemic, can building homes rebuild Australia?* AHURI Final Report No. 341. Australian Housing and Urban Research Institute Limited, www.ahuri.edu.au/research/finalreports/341

Salerno, J.P., Williams, N.D. and Gattamorta, K.A. (2020) 'LGBTQ populations: psychologically vulnerable communities in the COVID-19 pandemic'. *Psychological Trauma: Theory, Research, Practice, and Policy*, 12(S1): S239–42.

Tsai, J. and Wilson, M. (2020) 'COVID-19: a potential public health problem for homeless populations'. *The Lancet Public Health*, 5(4): e186–7.

van der Merwe, J. and Doucet, B. (2021) 'Housing challenges, mid-sized cities and the COVID-19 pandemic: critical reflections from Waterloo Region'. *Canadian Planning and Policy*, 2021(01): 70–90.

Vilenica, A., McElroy, E., Ferreri, M., Fernández Arrigoitia, M., García-Lamarca, M. and Lancione, M. (2020) 'COVID-19 and housing struggles: the (re) makings of austerity, disaster capitalism, and the no return to normal'. *Radical Housing Journal*, 2(1): 9–28.

Willsher, K. and Harrap, C. (2020) 'In a Paris banlieue, coronavirus amplifies years of inequality'. *The Guardian*, April 25.

World Health Organization (WHO) (2020) *WHO Director-General's opening remarks at the media briefing on COVID-19 – 5 March 2020*, www.who.int/director-general/speeches/detail/who-director-general-s-opening-remarks-at-the-media-briefing-on-COVID-19---5-march-2020

PART I

Housing Markets, Systems, Design, and Policies

TWO

Is COVID-19 a Housing Disease? Housing, COVID-19 Risk, and COVID-19 Harms in the UK

Rebecca Tunstall

Introduction

A hundred years ago, when infectious diseases were the principal threat to life expectancy, housing was at the center of public health initiatives in the UK and in other now-high-income countries. Links between poor housing and poor health have continued, despite decades of improvements in average housing conditions and substantial public investment. While the UK has relatively good-quality housing by international standards, polluted air shortens 40,000 lives and costs the National Health Service (NHS) £20bn annually, and housing health and safety risks cost the NHS £1.4bn a year (Nicol et al, 2016). In 2017–18 deaths were 49,000 higher in winter than summer, partly due to cold housing (Office for National Statistics (ONS), 2018). Eight hundred people died sleeping rough in England and Wales in 2019, at a mean age of 46 (ONS, 2020c). Reductions in housing allowances in 2012 caused about 26,000 extra cases of medium-term mental health conditions (Reeves et al, 2016).

Across the world, COVID-19 has returned housing to the forefront of public health. In both high-income nations and those with many crowded informal settlements, it is feared that shared accommodation, overcrowding, and large households have made self-isolation difficult or impossible. Overcrowding and housing insecurity have been associated with higher national cases in high- and medium-income countries (Shadmi et al, 2020; Brown et al, Chapter Ten; Xavier, Chapter Seven). Housing has also been central to lockdown experiences and to potential lockdown harms – to education, physical and mental health, working life, relationships, disposable income, and housing security. Home can be a place of harm as well as a refuge (Gurney, 2020). A politician from Newham, an area of London which in May 2020 had the highest COVID-19 death rate in the UK as well as amongst the worst overcrowding, declared, 'This is a housing disease' (Barker and Heath, 2020).

This chapter examines evidence from the UK to assess whether COVID-19 and lockdown harms are 'housing diseases'. While the UK has relatively good-quality housing, it has relatively high-income inequality, and a minority have poor-quality or very unaffordable homes. Over the 2000s and 2010s, the housing safety net has been weakened, with reduced eligibility and generosity of rent allowances, and less social housing. In addition, the UK has had among the highest COVID-19 death rates in the world (Johns Hopkins Coronavirus Resource Centre, 2021). There was a national lockdown across the UK over March–June 2020. In England, this was followed by a series of regional restrictions, a second lockdown in November and a third starting in December 2020. There were slightly different measures in other parts of the UK.

The links between housing and COVID-19 infection and death

UK data on COVID-19 cases and deaths are not usually linked to information on the housing conditions of the individual concerned, which makes it difficult to research the effects of housing. However, several UK studies have shown strong links between deprivation in people's home neighborhoods and the risk of death from COVID-19, even after controls (Public Health England (PHE), 2020). After controls including comorbidity, people in the most deprived 20 percent of neighborhoods had 1.75 times the risk of a confirmed COVID-19 death in hospital by the end of April than those in the least deprived 20 percent (OpenSAFELY, 2020). This is equivalent to the increased risk of being Black, obese, or having various serious diseases in the last year. Neighborhood deprivation also played a greater role in death rates for COVID-19 than in other deaths (PHE, 2020). Deprivation is partly a proxy for income, but also describes housing: the measure includes homelessness, overcrowding, affordability, and housing quality. Up to mid-April, there were very strong correlations between local authority age-standardized death rates and local housing conditions, including overcrowding, flats, rented housing, and large households (author's calculations). However, over time the virus spread into more varied localities and into care homes, and these correlations weakened. Nonetheless, most epidemiological models assume that large, mixed-age, or overcrowded households have increased risks of intra-household infection. Housing inequalities appear to have contributed to COVID-19 inequalities, for example, to the differences in death rates between ethnic groups in the UK (PHE, 2020). Overcrowded households were less likely to follow lockdown guidelines (Fancourt et al, 2020).

Further research is needed into the extent to which COVID-19 is a housing disease, in the sense of being demonstrably caused by housing conditions. However, housing is also playing a role in other ongoing harms from the disease itself and measures to contain it.

Being at home in lockdown

From March 23, 2020, people in the UK were told to 'stay at home'. In this first national lockdown, most people were at home for 23 or more hours a day. Forty-one percent did not go out at all for five or more days a week (Fancourt et al, 2020). Seventy-nine percent of social renters could not work because their jobs could not be done at home (or because of lack of childcare), compared to 59 percent of private renters and 50 percent of those with mortgages (Judge and Pacitti, 2020). However, 42 percent of those working were working at home (ONS, 2020a). They were also studying at home, caring for children at home (95 percent of children were not at school), and doing more unpaid caring for adults at home. All epidemiological models assume that people will get infected at home. Five percent of COVID-19-linked deaths and 20 percent of excess deaths by the end of May occurred at home. People also stayed at home ill: in March–June 2020 there were 56 percent fewer elective hospital admissions than over the same period in 2019.

Lockdown and other restrictions, school closure, and ongoing homeworking meant people have been doing more activities at home than usual, and have been exposed to their homes for many more waking hours than normal. Shortage of space and poor quality will have had greater impact (Hubbard, Chapter Four). People in overcrowded homes had worse mental health during lockdown (Fancourt et al, 2020). Seven percent of home-schoolers were struggling due to lack of quiet space. Ten percent of people said their well-being was affected by too much time with their household, and 15 percent said it was affected by too much time alone (ONS, 2020a). The impact on education and mental health may not be fully felt for years.

The effects of employment and income disruption on housing security

Housing has become a bigger and more problematic part of UK household budgets over the 2000s and 2010s. Half of working-age people had all real income growth over the period taken by increased housing costs (Clarke et al, 2016). Twenty-one percent of people in the UK had no savings going into the pandemic, and 22 percent had used their savings up after a month (Kempson and Poppe, 2020). By April 2020, 25 percent of households had lost income (ONS, 2020a). Forty percent thought it was likely that they would have serious money problems such as not being able to pay for housing, and 7 percent were in rent or mortgage arrears (ONS, 2020a; 2020b).

In March, the UK housing minister Robert Jenrick said that no one should be evicted because of rent arrears due to COVID-19. From March, there were moratoria on evictions and repossessions, initially for three months and later extended to the end of September (Wilson, 2021). Evictions cases began in September, but court capacity was reduced and there was another break over Christmas. Thus the potential effect of COVID-19 debts on housing security has been postponed. However, even before the pandemic, large proportions of people in the UK had high housing cost burdens, so that even small income drops could mean problems paying for housing, or material deprivation.

If social renters lose income, they are eligible for support with living and housing costs from the welfare state though Universal Credit (UC), which pays the whole rent for those on low income. People who own their homes outright generally have low housing costs, and many are of pensionable age with stable incomes. It is private renters and mortgaged homeowners, making up 19 percent and 29 percent respectively of all households in England in 2018–19, who are at most risk from income drops.

Private renters – Most private renters in England have tenancies that mean they can be asked to leave without arrears or any other misbehavior, and courts must automatically grant landlords possession once eight weeks' arrears have built up. By May, 5 percent of private renters working before lockdown had lost their jobs, 15 percent had been furloughed, and 12 percent had lost hours or income (Judge and Pacitti, 2020). Thirteen percent were behind with rent. Ten percent had tried to negotiate with landlords, but only 5 percent were successful (Judge, 2020). In June, another survey found that that 3 percent of private renters had built up arrears, and 2 percent had been threatened with eviction. By July, 36 percent of private sector renters had lost 20 percent or more income. A survey of landlords found that 13 percent of private tenants had not paid rent as normal, and 55 percent of landlords planned to absorb losses from at least one tenant.

Private renters whose incomes fall to low levels can claim support for living and housing costs through UC. However, this pays in full only the cheapest 30 percent of private rents in the local area. Before the pandemic, this meant 25 percent of renters claiming UC were unable to cover all their rent and had to make up the shortfall somehow. For those who made UC claims during the pandemic, 42 percent had shortfalls. Full data are not yet available, but when the moratorium on evictions ended in September, 'significant volumes' of cases started (ONS, 2020d).

Home owners – By April, 29 percent of mortgaged homeowner households had lost income (ONS, 2020b). By May, 3 percent of mortgaged owners in work before the pandemic had lost their jobs, 11 percent had been furloughed, and 15 percent had lost hours or income, and 8 percent were behind with housing costs (Judge, 2020). Homeowners who lose income can apply for UC for living costs, but not for housing costs. The number of UC claims with no housing entitlement, mainly made by owners with a mortgage, rose in the period March–May by 90 percent, to 1.9m across the UK.

In March, the government announced that mortgage providers should provide a three-month 'holiday' for mortgage holders in difficulties, later extended to six months. This 'holiday' is in effect extra borrowing which will result in higher or more extended payments. By November, 23 percent of mortgage holders, or 2.6m households, had arranged holidays (Wilson et al, 2020). These households had to find additional income before the holiday ended, or face arrears and potential repossession. Again, when repossessions restarted in September, 'significant volumes' of cases started (ONS, 2020d).

Thus COVID-19 is a disease which exposes the vulnerability of the UK housing system, and millions of homes and households, to employment and income shocks.

Homelessness in lockdown

Over April–September 2020, 20,000 mostly family households in England were accepted by their local authorities as homeless and with a statutory right to housing provision, 17 percent higher than the same period in 2019 (Ministry of Housing Communities and Local Government (MHCLG), 2021, MD1). Over January–March 2020, there were 88,000 households in temporary accommodation in England. By April–May the number had grown to 92,000, and by July–Sept it was 98,000 (MHCLG, 2021, TA1). These increases were part of a pre-existing trend. The moratorium on evictions and repossessions was not enough to prevent significant home loss.

Most single people are not eligible for statutory local authority support, meaning that some end up on the streets. As the first UK lockdown began, there was widespread concern that rough sleepers couldn't isolate – and might infect others. The government started a program to bring them into emergency accommodation, initially identifying 5,400 needing housing in England (Cromarty, 2020). The majority were in London. Over April–June, authoritative data based on daily records of Non-Governmental Organization (NGO) outreach workers showed that 80 percent of all rough sleepers in London identified over the period were booked into emergency accommodation, and 30 percent fewer were sleeping rough consistently (five or more times over three or more weeks) compared to the previous quarter (Combined Homelessness and Information Network (CHAIN), 2020). However, this was not the 100 percent reduction in homelessness policy makers promised. In addition, lockdown resulted in 77 percent more people found sleeping rough for the first time in April–June, compared to the same period in 2019 (CHAIN, 2020). Rough sleepers had much higher confirmed case rates than the general population (PHE, 2020). Thus COVID-19 seems to be a homelessness disease (see also Turman et al, Chapter Sixteen).

Conclusion

A close relationship between housing and COVID-19 infection seems intuitive, and is widely assumed. In practice the link is complex, and not easy to prove using available data. However, there is already strong evidence that in the UK, COVID-19 is a housing disease when it comes to lockdown harms. COVID-19 has placed the UK housing system, labor market, and welfare state under enormous strain, and has exposed significant weaknesses. COVID-19 has resulted in a big increase in street homelessness. The harms of home loss and material deprivation due to people trying to meet housing costs have not yet crystalized but seem likely to do so. There is also already similar evidence from other countries, including the US, Australia, and Italy.

A different housing system in the UK, with fewer households in the at-risk tenures of mortgaged home ownership and private renting, improved affordability, greater security for private renters, more generous rent allowances, and less homelessness would have meant less COVID-19 risk and harm. Researchers in the US and other countries have made the same points about their systems (see Hubbard, Chapter Four; Kayanan et al, Chapter Seventeen). Now, the UK urgently needs a plan to write off rent arrears or to help tenants pay. Local authorities need extra support to prevent evictions, rough sleeping, and family homelessness due to loss of wages. Some landlords may need support to cover rent losses. Housing developers, particular those of affordable housing, need encouragement to return to building.

On the other hand, housing could be central to what the OECD (Organisation for Economic Co-operation and Development) calls 'building back better', in the UK and worldwide (OECD, 2020). Improving existing housing and building high-quality new homes would create jobs, contribute to GDP, and reduce CO_2. Post-COVID-19, fewer people will be sure of secure, mortgageable jobs, and the welfare system will struggle to provide long-term supplementary or alternative income, and there may be further pandemics. This means it is essential to have greater numbers of more secure, affordable, healthy homes. This would improve the resilience of the housing system and the support it provides to the economy. It would increase disposable income, and reduce the risk of deprivation, mental illness, and homelessness linked to high housing costs.

References

Barker, N. and Heath, N. (2020) 'Council with highest COVID-19 death rate brands illness a "housing disease"'. *Inside Housing*, May 29.

Clarke, S., Corlett, A. and Judge, L. (2016) *The housing headwind: The impact of rising housing costs on UK living standards*. London: Resolution Foundation.

Combined Homelessness and Information Network (CHAIN) (2020) *Rough sleeping in London (CHAIN reports)*, https://data.london.gov.uk/dataset/chain-reports

Cromarty, H. (2020) *Coronavirus: support for rough sleepers (England)*. Briefing paper no. 09057, November 27, London: House of Commons Library.

Fancourt, D., Hei, W.M., Feifei, B. and Steptoe, A. (2020) *COVID-19 social study: results releases 1–11*, London: University College London.

Gurney, C. (2020) *Out of harm's way? Critical remarks on harm and the meaning of home during the 2020 COVID-19 social distancing measures*, April 8, UK Collaborative Centre for Housing Research.

Johns Hopkins Coronavirus Resource Centre (2021) https://coronavirus.jhu.edu/data/mortality

Judge, L. (2020) *Coping with housing costs during the coronavirus crisis: flash findings from the Resolution Foundation's coronavirus survey*, May 30, London: Resolution Foundation.

Judge, L. and Pacitti, C. (2020) *The Resolution Foundation housing outlook*, London: Resolution Foundation.

Kempson, E. and Poppe, C. (2020) *Coronavirus financial impact tracker*, Edinburgh: Standard Life Foundation.

Ministry of Housing Communities and Local Government (MHCLG) (2021) *Statutory homelessness live tables*, www.gov.uk/government/statistical-data-sets/live-tables-on-homelessness

Nicol, N., Roys, M. and Garrett, H. (2016) *The cost of poor housing to the NHS*, BRE.

Office for National Statistics (ONS) (2018) *Excess winter mortality in England and Wales: 2017 to 2018 (provisional) and 2016 to 2017 (final)*, Newport: ONS.

ONS (2020a) *Coronavirus and the social impacts on Great Britain: June 5, 2020*, Newport: ONS.

ONS (2020b) *Personal and economic well-being in Great Britain: May 2020*, Newport: ONS.

ONS (2020c) *Deaths of homeless people in England and Wales: 2019 registrations*, Newport: ONS.

ONS (2020d) *Mortgage and landlord possession statistics: July to September 2020*, Newport: ONS.

OpenSAFELY Collaborative (2020) 'OpenSAFELY: factors associated with COVID-19-related hospital death in the linked electronic health records of 17 million adult NHS patients'. *MedRxiv*, May 7.

Organisation for Economic Co-operation and Development (OECD) (2020) *Building back better: a sustainable, resilient recovery after COVID-19*, June 5, www.oecd.org/coronavirus/policy-responses/building-back-better-a-sustainable-resilient-recovery-after-COVID-19-52b869f5/

Public Health England (PHE) (2020) *Disparities in the risk and outcomes of COVID-19*, London: PHE.

Reeves, A., Clair, A., McKee, M. and Stuckler, D. (2016) 'Reductions in the United Kingdom's government housing benefit and symptoms of depression in the low-income households'. *American Journal of Epidemiology*, 184(6): 421–9.

Shadmi, E. et al (2020) 'Health equity and COVID-19: global perspectives'. *International Journal of Health Equity*, 19(104): np.

Wilson, W. (2021) *Coronavirus: support for landlords and tenants*. Briefing paper no. 08867, January 10, London: House of Commons Library.

Wilson, W., Cromarty, H. and Barton, C. (2020) *Mortgage arrears and repossessions (England)*. Briefing paper no. 04769, November 17, London: House of Commons Library.

THREE

De-Gentrification or Disaster Gentrification? Debating the Impact of COVID-19 on Anglo-American Urban Gentrification

Derek Hyra and Loretta Lees

According to Richard Florida, the self-styled urbanist who has made his fortune off the back of creative gentrification, New York City (NYC) and London are still buys – 'This is not the end of cities',[1] he recently proclaimed. Indeed, he sees the pandemic (and Black Lives Matter) as presenting an opportunity to 'reshape cities in more equitable ways'. He seems to want his cake and to eat it too?

In this chapter we consider two debates over the future of gentrification in the Anglo-American post-COVID-19 city: de-gentrification versus disaster gentrification. In one gentrification is killed off or goes into decline and we start to experience a post-gentrification city. In the other capital exploits the situation and gentrification continues, even grows. The former predicts doom for the center of Anglo-American cities, as the gentrifier classes move out to the suburbs or small towns or rural locations; the latter predicts the continuation of ongoing waves of gentrification that find ever more creative ways to exploit the urban. The question becomes: post-COVID-19, will gentrification die a sudden death or will it continue as usual, exploiting new niches and mutating as it has done before?

De-gentrification (death of the city)?

There have been proclamations about the demise or death of gentrification since at least the early 1990s. As Neil Smith (1996: 93) said: 'After the stretch-limo optimism of the 1980s was rear-ended in the financial crash of 1987, then totaled by the onset of economic depression two years later, real estate agents and urban commentators quickly began deploying the language of "de-gentrification" to represent the apparent reversal of urban change in the 1990s'. Smith echoed what *The New York Times* had said:

> In some corners of the city, the experts say, gentrification may be remembered along with junk bonds, stretch limousines and television evangelism, as just another grand excess of the 1980s ... As the dust settles, we can see that the areas that underwent a dramatic turnaround had severe limitations. Rich people are simply not going to live next to public housing. (Lueck, 1991)

Even Peter Marcuse (1993) mooted that de-gentrification was happening in the Lower East Side of NYC, or what he somewhat distastefully called 'plebeianization'. But as Lees and Bondi (1995) showed, these NYC predictions of de-gentrification did not happen, and the process took off even more aggressively following the 1987 recession. Over a decade later after the 2008 crash there were new predictions of de-gentrification both in North America and in Europe, but as Hochstenbach and Musterd (2018) argue the crisis impacted gentrification processes but it did *not* lead to de-gentrification.

In 2020 with a global pandemic and the onset of national and indeed global economic recession, the media began yet again mooting de-gentrification. The *Financial Times* in London (2020) asked: 'Could coronavirus spell the end of trendy east London?'. In NYC, there were some signs that gentrification might be slowing down. For instance, there appeared to be an increased preference among some New Yorkers for a suburban yard, porch, and space to socially distance and decompress.[2] In once red hot Manhattan, home and rental real estate prices year over year (August 2019 to August 2020) were slightly down and vacancy rates up,[3] while property values remained high and increasing in certain NYC suburban areas, where single-family housing supply is low and demand is high.[4] Is this the end of gentrification in the inner cities of say London and NYC?

Previous predictions of de-gentrification off the back of economic downturns have been far off the mark, as Hyra et al (2020) argue – in the US a fifth wave of gentrification (2010–20) was set up in part *by* the Great Recession (2007–09) and the racial inequality and financial rental housing shift it created. Our fear is that the COVID-19 recession will eventually do the same as the Great Recession in the US and the UK. The way the US is allocating small business loans ($659 billion worth) in the Paycheck Protection Program (PPP)[5] as well as the current home lending environment with historically low interest rates, and the deep-pocket investors' desires to buy low and sell high in certain minority rental markets,[6] is guaranteeing growing racial inequality as we move to the recovery period. This could trigger a sixth wave of US gentrification, 2020–30, which will take place disproportionately in Southern US cities, like Atlanta, Memphis, Birmingham, and Austin, where homebuying surged, compared to other US cities, among Millennials during the 2020 summer months.[7]

In the UK after the 2008 recession the financial aspect of housing survived the economic turmoil with the help of the state. To some degree this is because the UK (at least up until now) has been less prone to financialization than say the US

(Madden and Marcuse, 2016) and the state supports the rentier class and will, we surmise, do everything it can to protect private property. If we follow the 2008 scenario, gentrification will continue as usual and the housing crisis will continue. But there is also the possibility that the UK becomes more prone to financialization, more attractive for certain large corporations post-Brexit, escalating inequalities and pressures even further. Despite some evidence of Londoners' seeking to move outside the city to smaller towns, commuter towns or areas where they have second homes in (keeping a pied-à-terre in London), Savills (2020)[8] has been bullish that 'London will remain one of the most desirable cities in the world to live in'. In particular, ultra-high net worth individuals (UHNWIs) are still very interested in the top end of the prime London market, one of the most exclusive in the world, and it seems that super- or ultra-gentrification is not going anywhere soon. And it is very possible that the new geographies of property wealth distribution will open up new gaps for new processes of gentrification.

Browsing tweets from NYC, we can already see recognition of what is opening up:

> I'm staying here because now that all the rich whiny shits are leaving, it will finally be cheap enough to live here. The artists are returning to Soho. Nature is healing.

And long-time Londoners, or below New Yorkers, remain committed to their cities:

> 4th generation here (kids are 5th on Manhattan and Brooklyn sides). We survived draft riots, municipal consolidation, 1918 influenza, black outs, school strikes, garbage strikes, droughts, financial crisis, Guliani etc. Can't leave.

At the same time if some people are leaving larger cities, what does this mean for gentrification in the rural areas, villages, towns, and smaller cities they might move to? In the London context there has been refocused marketing attention on commutable locations within a 70 minute commute time from London, and there is some property transactions evidence that this has become a trend.[9] Here the pandemic could well reshape geographies of gentrification further and reminds us that gentrification is no longer just confined to the inner-city of big cities like London and New York.

Disaster gentrification (the city is not dead yet)?

COVID-19 can be categorized as a disaster, and the gentrification literature tells us that 'disaster capitalism' (Klein, 2007 – calculated free market solutions to crises that exploit and exacerbate inequalities) feeds gentrification; for example, it was seen to have triggered a fourth wave of gentrification in New Orleans after Hurricane Katrina (see Lees et al, 2008). Of course there are nuances around disaster gentrification, as Arena (2012) says it goes beyond the neoliberal coercion Klein discusses; he points to the indirect role played by non-profits in controlling and channeling dissent, facilitating the rollout of the local policy red carpet for gentrification actors. While each city's unique political context will alter the paths of gentrification, there are some common features we see moving forward.

COVID-19 is a health and financial disaster that capitalism is quite likely to exploit to create disaster gentrifications. And it is this circumstance we would argue that is the most plausible. In the US the COVID-19 cases and deaths have been disproportionately concentrated in minority areas, where frontline workers are overly concentrated (Yearby and Mohapatra, 2020; Stevens, Chapter Eight). On top of the higher COVID-19 caseloads in financially precarious communities of color, residents are experiencing higher rates of service sector unemployment. The unprecedented unemployment is destabilizing people's ability to pay their rent.[10] Despite moratoria on evictions, real estate personnel are finding ways to move people out during the pandemic, and public and private capital is paused and ready to move into these vulnerable areas.[11]

We believe that rather than stalling, the gentrification engine is revving up and capitalists with deep financial pockets and the ability to acquire large low-interest loans are about to step on the preverbal gas pedal (Cole et al, 2020). The vulnerable small businesses and unemployed residents in their way will be driven from their communities only to be dropped off in other outlying underserved areas.[12] While a vaccine is being rolled out, real estate investors are prepping new 'patient' neighborhoods for drastic profiteering makeovers. The placemaking 'surgeries' will be conducted by public-private partnerships with policy devices such as Tax Increment Financing (TIFs) and Business Improvement Districts (BIDs) (Schaller, 2019), as well as private financial investment vehicles including Real Estate Investment Trusts (REITs) (Sullivan, 2018).

In London, the densest city in the UK, which initially had a lower infection rate than the rest of the UK, but then one of the highest as the virus mutated – the turn away from dense living has not been what some have mooted; indeed it has been seen as a good thing regarding social isolation. If anything, COVID-19 is forcing Londoners to make more and better use of their local communities and economies – local and independent shops are faring well and busy. Walking and cycling (gentrifier loves) have taken off (see Scott, Volume 3; Mayers, Volume 4). What might happen is more locally nucleated patterns of localized gentrifications across the city, and the escalations of those gentrifications already happening in smaller cities and towns, the suburbs and indeed the rural (as the urban-rural dichotomy continues to collapse, and indeed may be escalated by new modes of work post-COVID-19).

Conclusion

Gentrification like capitalism in the UK and the US will no doubt continue. A new (fifth in the UK and possibly sixth in the US), post-COVID-19 wave of gentrification is predicted to occur, one more closely connected to processes of financialization than ever before. Those with access to low-interest-rate debt and capital will buy up vulnerable businesses and rental buildings on the cheap and will package and resell them when/if the values return during the post-pandemic recovery.

The state, and its recovery policies, will no doubt increase gentrification pressures, telling us that economic recession means attracting investment no matter what the impacts are is a no-brainer. This new, unapologetic, state-led gentrification will have implications for 'survivability' (Lees et al, 2018) with respect to gentrification. As Naomi Klein says:

> The 'shock doctrine' is the political strategy of using large-scale crises to push through policies that system-atically deepen inequality, enrich elites, and undercut everyone else. In moments of crisis, people tend to focus on the daily emergencies of surviving that crisis, whatever it is, and tend to put too much trust in those in power. We take our eyes off the ball a little bit in moments of crisis.[13]

With new geographies of work and residence it is reasonable to expect that processes of gentrification will become more spread out and variegated, attenuating localized urban, suburban, and rural gentrifications. The new city might have a richer but also a poorer urban core, more extreme forms of wealth and poverty, but there is real potential to seize the offices and spaces left by office workers to house the less wealthy, before more wealthy creative types become the new shock troops of further gentrification in these 'innovation' spaces. Different forms of spatial capital (see Rerat and Lees, 2011) will become important to gentrifiers as walkability and cyclability becomes ever more desired. With the COVID-19 pandemic, and the forthcoming economic recovery, we predict gentrification is not dead. Rather it will reveal itself again in the not too distant future as disaster gentrification. We need to prepare policy interventions now to preserve affordable housing so that equitable development is achieved. Otherwise, the capitalists will turn the pandemic, and our cherished city neighborhoods, into another round of profits over people.

Notes

1. www.bloomberg.com/news/features/2020-06-19/cities-will-survive-pandemics-and-protests
2. www.theatlantic.com/health/archive/2020/06/pandemic-cities-moving-remote-work/613069/
3. www.elliman.com/resources/siteresources/commonresources/static%20pages/images/corporate-resources/q2_2020/rental-08_2020.pdf
4. https://abcnews.go.com/US/suburbs-booming-ny-dead-real-estate-professionals-insist/story?id=72818297
5. www.forbes.com/sites/tommybeer/2020/05/18/minority-owned-small-businesses-struggle-to-gain-equal-access-to-ppp-loan-money/#463816cc5de3
6. www.dwell.com/article/pandemic-housing-gentrification-d4115008
7. www.forbes.com/sites/advisor/2020/07/15/10-most-popular-cities-for-millennial-homebuyers-right-now/#766cf21d60a6
8. www.savills.co.uk/research_articles/229130/304130-0
9. www.savills.co.uk/research_articles/229130/304130-0
10. www.dwell.com/article/pandemic-housing-gentrification-d4115008
11. https://time.com/5820634/evictions-coronavirus/
12. www.washingtonpost.com/business/2020/07/31/ethnic-enclaves-gentrification-coronavirus/?arc404=true
13. www.vice.com/en_us/article/5dmqyk/naomi-klein-interview-on-coronavirus-and-disaster-capitalism-shock-doctrine

References

Arena, J. (2012) *Driven from New Orleans: How Non-Profits Betray Public Housing and Promote Privatization*. Minnesota: University of Minnesota Press.

Cole, H., Anguelovshi, I., Baró, F., García-Lamarca, M., Kotsila, P., Pérez del Pulgar, C., Shokry, G. and Triguero-Mas, M. (2020) 'The COVID-19 pandemic: power and privilege, gentrification, and urban environmental justice in the global north'. *Cities & Health*, 1–5, DOI: 10.1080/23748834.2020.1785176

Hochstenbach, C. and Musterd, S. (2018) 'Gentrification and the suburbanization of poverty: changing urban geographies through boom and bust periods'. *Urban Geography*, 39(1): 26–53.

Hyra, D., Fullilove, M., Moulden, D. and Silva, K. (2020) *Contextualizing gentrification chaos: the rise of the fifth wave.* Working paper, Washington, DC: The Metropolitan Policy Center.

Klein, N. (2007) *The Shock Doctrine: The Rise of Disaster Capitalism.* London: Allen Lane.

Lees, L., Annunziata, S. and Rivas-Alonso, C. (2018) 'Resisting planetary gentrification: the value of survivability in the fight to stay put'. *Annals of the Association of American Geographers*, 108(2): 346–55.

Lees, L. and Bondi, L. (1995) 'De-gentrification and economic recession: the case of New York City'. *Urban Geography*, 16(3): 234–53.

Lees, L., Slater, T. and Wyly, E. (2008) *Gentrification.* New York: Routledge.

Lueck, T.J. (1991) 'Prices decline as gentrification ebbs: the future is uncertain in areas that bloomed too late in the 1980s'. *The New York Times*, September 29, Section 10.

Madden, D. and Marcuse, P. (2016) *In Defense of Housing: The Politics of Crisis.* London: Verso Books.

Marcuse, P. (1993) 'Degentrification and advanced homelessness: new patterns, old processes'. *Netherlands Journal of Housing and the Built Environment*, 8(2): 177–91.

Rerat, P. and Lees, L. (2011) 'Spatial capital, gentrification and mobility: lessons from Swiss core cities'. *Transactions of the Institute of British Geographers*, 36(1): 126–42.

Schaller, S. (2019) *Business Improvement Districts and the Contradictions of Placemaking.* Georgia: University of Georgia Press.

Smith, N. (1996) 'After Tompkins Square Park: degentrification and the revanchist city', in A.D. King (ed) *Re-Presenting the City.* London: Palgrave, pp 93–107.

Sullivan, E. (2018) *Manufactured Insecurity.* Berkeley, CA: University of California Press.

Yearby, R. and Mohapatra, S. (2020) 'Law, structural racism, and the COVID-19 pandemic'. *Journal of Law and the Biosciences*, 1–20, https://papers.ssrn.com/sol3/papers.cfm?abstract_id=3612824

FOUR

'Living in a Glass Box': The Intimate City in the Time of COVID-19

Phil Hubbard

Introduction

> Quarantining and self-isolating people in their homes can change the habitational dynamics, rhythms and politics of the home. Restricting people to their homes in this way presents a wide-ranging suite of issues and challenges. In some cases it puts lives in danger. (Rogers and Power, 2020: 178)

Joanne was an asset manager in London, living in a flat in one of the many new-build riverfront developments in the Battersea and Nine Elms areas of South London. She moved into the development in 2019, attracted by the proximity to her place of work, a profusion of local bars and restaurants but also the on-site facilities, a concierge, and gym among them. But during the lockdown of 2020, her attitude to her home changed. "I spent seven weeks isolated there and realized that I absolutely hated it," she recounted, continuing, "When you take away all the amenities that these developments adver-tise, then you realize you're just living in a glass box". Come the summer, Joanne sold her flat, pooled resources with her partner, and bought a detached house in Datchworth Green, Hertfordshire, some 30 miles out of the capital (www.bbc.co.uk/news/business-53670199).

Joanne's case suggests that the quote from Rogers and Power at the beginning of the chapter about the impact of isolation has more than a ring of truth to it. Moreover, Joanne's case is far from isolated. During lockdown, property agents revealed that there had been a surge of interest among Londoners for properties elsewhere. More than half of the online property searches were for homes in rural locations, with Rightmove reporting that searches for houses with gardens reached an all-time high in April 2020. For some, this was no doubt about cashing in on the inflated prices of London property compared with the rest of the country (Hamnett and Reades, 2019). In 2009 just one percent of Londoners leaving the capital left to live in the north of the country, but by 2019 this had reached 13 percent with the larger cheaper homes available around 'buzzing' northern cities like Leeds and Newcastle proving a particular draw (Booth and Campbell, 2019). But for many looking to move out of London post-lockdown it appeared the sentiments they were expressing were ones akin to those voiced by Joanne: lockdown meant they simply wanted a bigger home with more outdoor space (see also Hyra and Lees, Chapter Three).

Though it is too early to conclude what the comparative impact of lockdown on mental and physical well-being for those living in different forms of housing, all the evidence to date suggests that experiences of lockdown in the UK were markedly different for those living with no outdoor space compared with those who have gardens or somewhere they can get fresh air and exercise (see Tunstall, Chapter Two; Brown et al, Chapter Ten; Warnock, Chapter Twelve; Kayanan et al, Chapter Seventeen, all this volume). But for some, added to this has been the challenge of combining homeworking and everyday living in homes that are simply not large enough to accommodate both. During the COVID-19 lockdown, some 52 percent of working-age adults (or over 15 million people) were estimated to be homeworking compared with the 1.7 million usually thought to do so. Commissioning a YouGov panel survey of 1,000 Londoners during lockdown (April 2020) we found this figure was higher in London, at around 70 percent – a not particularly surprising finding given the prominence of public administration, finance, insurance, law, advertising, and related 'creative' industries in the city.

Our survey focused on the degree to which the YouGov panel respondents were satisfied with homeworking, using a five-point scale (very satisfied, fairly satisfied, neutral, fairly unsatisfied, or very unsatisfied) and then asking them to list what they saw as its main advantages and disadvantages. One of the more interesting findings was that those living in detached homes in London were four times more likely to report being very satisfied with homeworking than those living in flats or apartments in purpose-built blocks (chi square = 23.744, df = 17, p = 0.070). Of those living in properties with four rooms or fewer, 64 percent reported being very dissatisfied with working at home, as opposed to 35 percent of those living in properties with five or more rooms. Of those in smaller properties, 70 percent reported difficulties in drawing boundaries between home and working life, as opposed to 30 percent in larger ones (chi square = 4.994, df = 1, p = 0.025). All of this implies that those living in smaller properties, especially flats, are less happy to be homeworking than those living in larger homes, even when allowing for other factors such as social class, gender, age, or the presence of children. Here, we were told that the challenges included lack of a workstation, poor thermal comfort, and ambient noise, but by far the most cited problem was that of lack of privacy: those working at home alongside others reported great difficulty in demarcating a working space, and many reported working propped up in bedrooms, or retreating to communal hallways and fire escapes when videoconferencing (see Hubbard et al, 2020). Clearly, for those working at home, life in smaller homes was problematic during lockdown.

Privacy, intimacy, and the post-COVID-19 home

Privacy can be defined as the intentional separation of self from society which helps maintain identity, integrity, and personality (Altman, 1975). It is not about solitude or seclusion per se – although it can be – but rather the ability that people have to keep their thoughts, feelings, and actions to themselves at the same time as they can choose whether or not to admit those of others. Privacy is a 21st-century preoccupation, and a concept frequently invoked in academic debates about state surveillance, data security, and media intrusion. Intimacy is related to, but distinct from, privacy. It concerns the forms of closeness and connection that are associated with moments of self-disclosure, including the forms of emotional openness associated with sexual and familial relationships. While intimacy is increasingly mediated (via virtual technologies and e-communication), it continues to be assumed that intimacy is facilitated by physical proximity, and that there is an important equation between home life and intimate life. Questions of intimacy are hence central to ongoing debates concerning the relation of gender, sexuality, and space as they pertain to housing (Hashim et al, 2006).

While the relationship between density, privacy, and health is not straightforward (Altman, 1975), it is clear that living in high-density, vertical developments can have negative consequences for people's health and well-being. As noted earlier, notions of thermal comfort, poor air circulation, and inappropriate facilities for food production/consumption are all major issues here. But the idea that such forms of dwelling might not allow for an adequate degree of privacy is surely a crucial one. Survey work in a range of cities in the Global North suggests those living in high-density, rented accommodation report the highest rates of neighbor nuisance, with as many as two out of three experiencing persistent problems (Cheshire et al, 2018). These issues are to do with sharing stairwells, lifts, and communal areas, and noise from neighbors above and below. But they are also to do with being overlooked: while there is an optics of power involved in overlooking others from on high, many vertical developments lack the type of privacy associated with more traditional suburban dwellings, which are shielded by hedges, fences, or walls. In short, most vertical dwellings are overlooked, and are hyper-visible, not least to other high-rise dwellers nearby.

Such constant awareness that one is sharing space, or living where there is frequent disturbance, can have significant impacts on well-being. For example, the reported effects of neighbor noise include hearing loss, stress, interrupted sleep, cognitive deficits, and poor physical and mental well-being (Evans et al, 2003). This is not just because of the physical qualities of the noise that crosses the boundaries between different housing units, but the fact it represents the unwanted and unavoidable receipt of the sound of other people's intimate lives. As Stokoe (2006: 3) argues, 'Neighbours can *hear* (and overhear) arguments, toilet flushes, children playing, music and television choices, sexual intercourse; they can *smell* next-door's dinner, painting, and pets; and they can *see* who comes and goes and at what time, who lives in the house, the type of house it is, and so on'. This suggests that privacy and intimacy are relational: if someone sees, hears, or smells the intimate lives of others, they too might feel unable to keep their own life adequately private, and modify their intimate behaviors (Morrison et al, 2013). This can have consequences for partnering and parenting, as well as rituals of self-care: for example, dressing, washing, cooking. Privacy, as much as space, comfort or security per se, should then be a priority for post-COVID-19 housing policy: we need homes that allow their occupants to achieve the privacy they need in lockdown and beyond.

Shrinking homes in London

At present, much is uncertain about the nature of the post-COVID-19 city, and whether we will ever inhabit cities in quite the same way again. But if working at home is to be the 'new normal', especially for the 'creative class' who can most readily do so, then one key implication of the evidence presented earlier is that we need to create decent homes where there is sufficient privacy to enable people to feel they can work without interruption. Likewise, it would seem sensible to design flat and apartment blocks where lifts, stairwells, and service areas are not shared by large numbers of people and social distancing is difficult. But this is the *inverse* of what has actually happened: the last decade has witnessed a headlong rush to fill London – and our other core cities – with 'micro-apartments' aimed at millennials, students, and key workers (Harris and Nowicki, 2020). This race to build a denser, compact city has been partly justified with reference to debates about health. Urban sprawl is bad, we are told, producing automobile-dependent populations who seldom walk and graze on drive-through fast food. In *Happy City*, Montgomery (2013) notes that the consensus appears to be that sprawl makes people unhappy and unhealthy. Yet Montgomery also warns against hyper-density, noting the problems of too much noise, not enough space and not enough solitude. This then is perhaps the key issue to be acknowledged when we think about housing post-COVID-19: we need housing that is both a working and living space, providing sufficient privacy to promote relaxation, recovery, a focus on work at some times and play at others.

The assertion that larger homes offering more privacy are better than smaller homes seems common-sensical given historical perceptions of higher-density and vertical housing have generally emphasized its association with social disadvantage. But, more recently, the privileged position of detached, suburban housing in the Global North has been challenged through renegotiations of the acceptability, and necessity, of higher-density living (Baker, 2013). In the expensive capital cities of the Global North in particular, a variety of factors – austerity, lack of affordable land, in-migration – are encouraging a move towards increasingly compact, high-density, vertical living, with much new-build in the form of 'micro-apartments' designed to appeal to young professionals (Gabbe, 2015). Some of these are well below the minimum apartment size allowed in the past, and have required revision of relevant building regulations: as a consequence, the average size of new-build flats is declining. Read charitably, such trends are in keeping with the tenets of sustainable urbanism, promoting compact, walkable and 'safe' cities characterized by street-level activity and vibrancy. Less generously, it could be argued that cities are succumbing to an energy-hungry vertical sprawl of poorly-designed apartments (Nethercote and Horne, 2019).

In the UK, the average size of new-build flats and apartments is thought to be declining rapidly: the average had already fallen to just 65 square meters by 2014, prompting new space standards in 2015 stipulating that a one-bed, one-room flat must be a minimum of 37 square meters. Yet despite this there is a perception that many flats and apartments in the capital are still below this recommended minimum size. Deregulatory planning reforms since 2013 have been partly to blame here, with the removal of the requirement for developers to apply for planning permission to convert an office building to a residential one (Ferm et al, 2020). The Conservative Party's 2020 mantra of 'build, build, build' – seeing the construction industry as one of the routes out of a post-COVID-19 recession – has further encouraged the construction of affordable housing by extending these permitted development rights (PRD) to abandoned shop units hit by the decline of High Street spending. Ferm et al (2020) suggest that since 2013 around 65,000 units of housing have been constructed via this PDR route, escaping any real scrutiny of minimum household size. Copley (2019) suggests 15,929 of these have been in London – but that only 71 (0.4 percent) of these were defined as genuinely affordable, and around 59 percent of these smaller than the stipulated minimum space standard.

This suggests that some developers are rushing to purchase office buildings, and turning these unsuitable premises into sub-size and sub-standard housing; 'filing cabinets for London's poor', in effect, with entire homes sometimes smaller than budget hotel rooms. Clifford et al undertook field visits to a range of schemes in those local authorities where PDR conversions of offices had been most prevalent – including Enfield in London – and concluded:

> Permitted development conversions do seem to create worse quality residential environments than planning permission conversions in relation to a number of factors widely linked to the health, wellbeing and quality of life of future occupiers. These aspects are primarily related to the internal configuration and immediate neighbouring uses of schemes, as opposed to the exterior appearance, access to services or broader neighbourhood location. In office-to-residential conversions, the larger scale of many conversions can amplify residential quality issues. (Clifford et al, 2020: 10)

The conclusion we might draw from this is that offices converted into small homes often make poor homes, being characterized by a lack of space, poor natural light, and little or no noise insulation.

But this potentially tells only part of the story. Our analysis of 2.8 million data records of sales price data for London (from the Land Registry, since 1995), when combined with 4 million Energy Performance Certificates containing estimates of housing size (with a match rate of around 60–80 percent per annum), shows around one in 20 homes in London violates the national minimum space requirements. These small flats cost, on average, in excess of £8,000 per square meter, making them relatively more expensive than homes that are around 100 square meters, which cost on average around £5,500 per square meter. This suggests that small homes are actually less affordable, meter for meter, than those homes that are more expensive. In part, this can be explained by the costs of installing bathrooms and kitchens, which are relatively consistent whether it is a one-, two- or three-bed property, but even so this points to the fact that not all small properties are cheap and that few are genuinely affordable. Indeed, in analyzing the data, we have found that more smaller properties are in inner London, including some of the least affordable locations in 'prime' London, but building activity (new small homes) are distributed relatively equally between inner and outer London.[1] Some, but not all, micro-apartment developments are in converted office blocks – and there is actually no significant correlation between permitted development rights and the location of micro-apartments. Our mapping of small homes suggests they are much more widespread than sometimes assumed. While much smaller, substandard housing is clearly for 'key workers' and low-income residents, with notable pockets in diverse multi-ethnic suburbs like Croydon and Deptford, there are also higher-spec developments targeting transnational migrants and those seeking investment opportunities in 'prime London'. For example, a one-bedroom studio of less than 30 square meters on the 23rd floor of the Pan Peninsula Tower, Canary Wharf, is on sale for £370,000. While barely big enough to swing a cat in, the development does promise a 24-hour concierge, communal cinema room, and access to the 48th-floor cocktail lounge. But the question remains: if lockdown becomes the new normal, do such glass boxes really constitute decent homes? Or do we need a fundamental rethinking of current housing standards to ensure that we find a middle ground between building more dense, small homes in the city center and the more sprawling, out-of-town homes that have suddenly become so attractive to Londoners?

As Rogers and Power (2020) conclude, COVID-19 has shed light on a UK housing system that is essentially broken, and moving forward the challenge may well be to offer more radical solutions which have a 'built-in' layer of intimacy that allows occupants of homes to connect with one another when they want, but cut each other off when they need to.

Note

[1] For maps, see www.kcl.ac.uk/research/no-space-like-home-the-geography-of-micro-apartments-in-london

References

Altman, I. (1975) *The Environment and Social Behavior: Privacy, Personal Space, Territory, and Crowding*. Monterey, CA: Brooks/Cole Publishing.

Baker, T. (2013) 'Home-making in higher density cities: residential experiences in Newcastle, Australia'. *Urban Policy and Research*, 31(3): 265–79.

Booth, R. and Campbell, L. (2019) 'Escaping the madness: steep rise in Londoners moving to northern Britain'. *The Guardian*, Feb 14, www.theguardian.com/uk-news/2020/feb/14/rising-tide-of-londoners-moving-to-northern-england

Cheshire, L., Fitzgerald, R. and Liu, Y. (2018) 'Neighbourhood change and neighbour complaints'. *Urban Studies*, DOI: 10.1177/0042098018771453

Copley, T. (2019) *Slums of the Future? Permitted Development Conversions in London*. London: London Assembly Labour.

Evans, G.W., Wells, N.M. and Moch, A. (2003) 'Housing and mental health: a review of the evidence and a methodological and conceptual critique'. *Journal of Social Issues*, 59(3): 475–500.

Ferm, J., Clifford, B., Canelas, P. and Livingstone, N. (2020) 'Emerging problematics of deregulating the urban: the case of permitted development in England'. *Urban Studies*, 1–19, DOI: 10.1177/0042098020936966

Gabbe, C.J. (2015) 'Looking through the lens of size: land use regulations and micro-apartments in San Francisco'. *Cityscape*, 17(2): 223–38.

Hamnett, C. and Reades, J. (2019) 'Mind the gap: implications of overseas investment for regional house price divergence in Britain'. *Housing Studies*, 34(3): 388–406.

Harris, E. and Nowicki, M. (2020) ' "Get smaller"? Emerging geographies of micro-living'. *Area*, 591–9, https://doi.org/10.1111/area.12625

Hashim, A.H., Rahim, Z.A., Rashid, S.N.S.A. and Yahaya, N. (2006) 'Visual privacy and family intimacy: a case study of Malay inhabitants living in two-storey low-cost terrace housing'. *Environment and Planning B: Planning and Design*, 33(2): 301–18.

Hubbard, P., Reades, J. and Walter, H. (2020) 'Viewpoint: shrinking homes, COVID-19 and the challenge of homeworking'. *Town Planning Review*, https://doi.org/10.3828/tpr.2020.46

Montgomery, C. (2013) *Happy City: Transforming Our Lives through Urban Design*. New York: Macmillan.

Morrison, C.A., Johnston, L. and Longhurst, R. (2013) 'Critical geographies of love as spatial, relational and political'. *Progress in Human Geography*, 37(4): 505–21.

Nethercote, M. and Horne, R. (2016) 'Ordinary vertical urbanisms: city apartments and the everyday geographies of high-rise families'. *Environment and Planning A*, 48(8): 1581–98.

Rogers, D. and Power, E. (2020) 'Housing policy and the COVID-19 pandemic: the importance of housing research during this health emergency'. *International Journal of Housing Policy*, 20(2): 177–83.

Stokoe, E. (2006) 'Public intimacy in neighbour relationships and complaints'. *Sociological Research Online*, 11(3): 1–21.

FIVE

Mardin Lockdown Experience: Strategies for a More Tolerant Urban Development

Zeynep Atas and Yuvacan Atmaca

The COVID-19 crises created a drastic confrontation with our urban, and housing environments. This chapter examines two very different parts of the city of Mardin, Turkey, one modern and one traditional, and how they dealt with the first wave of the pandemic. During the lockdown, the modern part of the city that was primarily developed through generic urban development patterns based on modernist infrastructure, went through a complete paralysis. The insufficient living conditions within its apartments and interrupted service provision emerged as the most problematic issues. On the other hand the historic parts of Mardin, built using traditional methods, sustained a healthier context, despite lacking many of the comforts of modern living and modern housing. Experiencing these differences in lockdown, the old city center's efficiency in dealing with the pandemic, compared with the ineffectiveness of more modern neighborhoods, evoked the need to explore the features of our cities that create more self-sufficient, and thus, tolerable living conditions in the COVID-19 era.

The urbanization of Turkey is generally analyzed in three consecutive periods that correspond to major social, political, economic, and spatial transformations: The Early Republican Era of 1920–50, the Post-War era of 1950–80, and the Neoliberal Era of post-1980 (Bozdogan, 2001, Akcan, 2012). The first period:

> was a scene for the emergence of the Turkish nation-state and the ambitious modernization efforts of the nationalist elite. The second period corresponds to the post-war era marked by popularization of politics and the unprecedented urban sprawl in Turkish cities, and finally, the post-1980 era reflects the integration of Turkey's economy into the neoliberal world market and the cultural effects of globalization. (Batuman, 2014: 270)

The first era was ideologically centered on creating a modern national identity from scratch, liberated from any bonds to the past, including the 600 years of the Ottoman era. Thus, socio-cultural modernization and its urban correspondence utilized Tabula Rasa[1] as a means of that ideology. Starting from the second era, though, with accelerated industrialization, increasing rural-urban migrations, and liberalization in economics, modern urban development could only become an urgent response to the housing problem of vast numbers of migrating populations. Leaving aside design and planning procedures along with the consideration of geography-specific natural, socio-cultural, and economic contexts, a mass sprawl of uniform urban development occurred during this era.

The new settlements of Mardin developed in this context as an agglomeration of uniform apartment blocks with standardized apartment units, ungrounded in terms of their relations with the existing local contexts. The old city center, on the other hand, developed for centuries through an accumulated knowledge that emerged as a combination of diverse natural, socio-cultural, and economic parameters specific to certain geographies. The extreme conditions of COVID-19 created an opportunity to realize and observe key features of our environments that appear to be efficient in dealing with crises. Although modern infrastructure has its benefits, the defects of modern developments came to surface during the first wave of the pandemic, especially due to their disengagement with their local context, resulting in high levels of reliance on service infrastructures. On the other hand, some features of traditional neighborhoods made them more con-ducive during a time of an immediate crisis, even despite their disadvantages in providing certain comforts of modern living. In this sense, tolerance through self-sufficiency emerged as a key compound that needs to be explored. This chapter aims to examine the efficient features of our living environments in relation to the contingency of city-making processes, in order to develop future visions for design and urban planning.

The city of Mardin: a historical background

Mardin is a historic city in south-east Turkey, on the Syrian border. Developed as a military post of the East Roman Empire, the historic architectural heritage of the city dates back to the 12th, 16th, and 19th centuries (Alioglu, 2000). The old city center was built with traditional stone buildings, terraced on a slope overlooking Mesopotamia Plain. The old city developed organically: interwoven along the topography, with narrow, shaded pathways *snuggling* through. This organic pattern is also manifested in the organic structure of the society built upon kinship, communality, and solidarity.

Geographical restrictions both for urban growth and the pene-tration of modern urban infrastructure, such as transportation, water, natural gas, and waste-collection, directed new devel-opment to the north-western plains in the 1980s (Çağlayan, 2016). Following the general urbanization trends noted earlier, the new settlements of Mardin developed in this period with generic housing estates and individual apartment blocks (Tekeli,

Figure 5.1: Mardin, new settlement (left) and the old city center (right)

Source: author's photograph

2009, Çağlayan, 2016). After the relocation of the administrative center to these new settlements at the end of the 1990s, they became popular living environments for the middle and upper classes, who were attracted to, and could afford a modern living (Çağlayan, 2016) (Figure 5.1).This resulted in the desolation of the traditional housing stock in the old city center by the owners. Together with accelerating immigration from rural areas in the late 1990s, the old city was left to middle- and lower-income groups, most of whom were tenants (Tuncer and Aksulu, 1993).

Meanwhile, the old city center was declared a historical preservation site in 1979, and listed in UNESCO's Temporary List of World Heritage in 2000 (Çağlayan, 2016). In parallel to government-led renovations, the housing stock within the neighborhoods was also transformed by user-made additions, resulting in the self-organized and unique architectural environment of today.

The socio-cultural and economic structure of the city has also transformed, especially with migrations. First came the rural-urban migration of the 1990s, which has been followed by an accelerating rate of immigration from Syria since 2011. Due to the existing socio-cultural diversity, lower rents, and prevailing local economics, the old city could absorb the effects of the immigration crisis more effectively. The diverse socio-cultural structure of the city, consisting of Turkish-Arabs, Kurds, and Assyrians, already created a tolerant environment. The ongoing economic structure in the old city of Mardin consisting of small-scale manufacturing workshops and small retailers sustained a flexible economic structure in which the refugees could take part, making use of their skills and know-how.

As a result of these developments, the new settlement became a more popular destination for more affluent residents, while the old city of Mardin, deprived of the comforts of modern living, and populated highly by lower-income groups, was considered to be a disadvantaged environment. However, COVID-19 reversed the situation in favor of the old city. Although very advantageous in service provision, during the first wave of the pandemic, the new settlement appeared to fail in relieving the psychological effects of the lockdown, such as feelings of imprisonment. The poor quality and generic designs of the apartments in the new settlements, and lack of involvement of natural assets in design and planning processes resulted in a less tolerant urban environment for residents. The old city, on the other hand, has challenging living conditions, such as freezing water, the difficulties of stove heating in winters, and the general lack of municipal services. However, during the pandemic, it provided a healthier and more comfortable living environment. This was as a result of its tolerant and self-sufficient spatial, socio-cultural, and economic structure.

A tolerant living environment: a comparison of the new settlement and the old city of Mardin

The concept of tolerance is interpreted here as the ability of our cities to cope with the unpredictable conditions created by crises, especially in terms of immediate responses upon first encounters. In this context, self-sufficiency of the living environment plays a crucial role. In the old city of Mardin, permeability of spatial, socio-cultural, and economic relations emerged as a result of the specific local context, and became the driving force in providing a more self-sufficient and tolerant environment. A comparison of the two different urban settings, the old city and the new settlement of Mardin, in COVID-19 lockdowns[2] through these concepts provides valuable insights for further discussions.

The old city center developed through organic patterns and could easily be perceived as a natural extension of its topography. The settlement is tightly interwoven and it is impossible to either identify or extricate *one house* from the whole. Each house consists of rectangular units of varying sizes and functions, organized horizontally following an L- or a U-shape, creating a unique spatial organization. The horizontal and vertical layout of these units through the topography, while forming inner courtyards, *eyvan*s,[3] and terraces, also enables permeability in both directions. The *dam* – rooftop – of one unit becomes the terrace of another on the upper part of the slope. The spatial permeability occurs on two levels: first, within the house and second, between the *outside* and the house. Closed, open, or semi-open spaces within houses – being *out* in the open air, while still staying *inside* the house – appeared to be one of the most important factors in alleviating the effects of the lockdown (Figure 5.2). Compared to the definitive borders of the apartments in the new settlement, where balconies became the only access to fresh air, sunlight, and social contact, the perception of confinement is reduced substantially. This was especially apparent for children who could maintain most of their daily recreation routines *in* and *out* of the house. Spatial permeability also strengthens the already-existing permeability of social relations. Pedestrian-oriented pathways of the old city act as an extension to the houses, or open spaces within the houses create visual and social contact between different households. Disturbing in normal times, generally creating an invasion of privacy, and community pressure on domestic life, visual permeability eased social interaction during the lockdowns. On the other hand, due to their spatial organization and disconnection to the existing topography, the apartment blocks of the new settlement are unable to provide the possibility of interaction with the surrounding open space (Figure 5.3).

Figure 5.2: Permeability of socio-spatial borders in the Old Settlement of Mardin

Source: author's photograph

Figure 5.3: New Settlement, built without regard for the local topography

Source: author's photograph

Another important factor in creating self-sufficient living is the house's integration to the urban economy. House, *oikos* in ancient Greek, was the core of ancient society and economy (Davies, 1992). In traditional means, the *house* is an *ecological* being, *housing* the family and means of domestic production (Davies, 1992; Cox, 1998). Within the persisting traditional living in the old city of Mardin, the house still maintains this basic role. Due to the living habits and availability of space, the house provides for vegetative and animal production, utilizing the endemic flora and fauna of the region. In comparison, the new settlements of Mardin are detached from land, and therefore connections to domestic food production; as a result, they are far more dependent on services and businesses.

The utilization of natural water resources is another factor in enabling self-sufficient living. The old city was built on a slope with underground water reserves. Composed of cisterns and wells within the houses, and fountains dispersed throughout the city, this ancient water infrastructure still supplies water for domestic use. In contrast with the new settlement, where drinking water is supplied from the supermarkets, permanent and first-hand access becomes a major relief especially in the first encounter with a crisis like COVID-19.

The self-sufficient living in the old city is also supported by the prevailing local social network and economy. The organic socio-cultural structure that is built upon kinship, solidarity, and strong neighborhood relations creates a sense of communal support in any crisis. On the other hand, the introverted apartment living characteristic of new settlements, generates individuality and appears to be disadvantageous when the support of a communal body becomes a relief. Facilitated by these organic and permeable social relations, prevailing local economics also enables immediate access to basic needs if required: the baker, the butcher, or the grocer are neighbors or an acquaintance of a neighbor. Relying mostly on a high number of national chain stores which operate on an institutional level instead of personal initiation, the new settlement is less efficient in sustaining the immediate needs of its inhabitants in a crisis.

All these factors that maintain a tolerant urban living environment depend on the active involvement of citizens in both the processes of city-making and the utilization of the features of an urban environment. Tolerance in an urban sense involves the capacity of our cities for self-organization: a thousand years of practiced ability of humanity to take personal or communal initiation, in creating our social, cultural, political, economic, and urban system in the first place (De Landa, 2003). It is a practiced ability, although active in local contexts, loosened by the service-dependent systems. And it has become one of the main forces in the COVID-19 crisis, performing within the existing system, to empower the self-sufficiency of our living environments.

Conclusion

During the COVID-19 lockdowns, the boundaries of our homes and immediate neighborhoods became the limits of our daily lives. Locked up in our houses, we realized what basics make a living environment healthy in both the physiological and psychological sense: accessibility to fresh air, sunlight, food, natural resources, and social network even in a limited sense. Thus, the necessity of living in urban environments providing for these basics has now become more apparent (see also Hubbard, Chapter Four). The processes of city-making therefore need to be reconsidered to generate urban systems tolerant enough to sustain the basics of living under certain restrictions. In this context, relative self-sufficiency and independence from service infrastructures appear to be vital. A comprehensive and place-specific interpretation of the notion of permeability in spatial, socio-cultural, and economic means necessitate more self-sufficient environments that are grounded in the immanent, accumulated knowledge of the place.

The comparison of the new and the old settlement of Mardin in this sense demonstrates some key features to be involved in more tolerant future urban development strategies: engagement with the topographic conditions and a reconsideration of the definitive borders of apartment blocks to create permeability between the indoor and outdoor spaces; utilization of the existing natural resources; flexible policies for spatial, socio-cultural, and economic organization to allow self-organization, personal, and communal initiation while reducing service-dependency; urban economic development considering and supporting local capacities.

Those limited number of strategies that could vary depending on the local contexts, could make way for a more grounded, thus, tolerant living environment. Perhaps, the main deficiency of urban strategies in Turkey has been the disengagement from the existing local knowledge, and intolerance towards the self-organizational nature of the being. Living through an age of crises, especially this very short period of the one brought about by COVID-19, it becomes an even more urgent task to shift our approach to our living environment. Immanent geographic, socio-cultural, and economic know-ledge of a place is accumulated over centuries and emerged and developed through our harmonious *coexistence* with the earth. Ignoring this knowledge is no less than cutting off that vital relationship. Traditional environments, still embodying that knowledge, present us with an opportunity to re-discover and re-evaluate. It is not about praising the traditional, or an impossible restoring of the old. But instead of 'a colossal and shapeless agglomeration' (Lefebvre, 1996: 148), developing *contingent* urban development strategies that are grounded in the existing dynamics of life.

Notes

[1] The concept of Tabula Rasa dates back to Aristotle but with John Locke it has gained its modern interpretation as the philosophical idea of Blank slate (Tournikiotis, 1999). In 20th-century modernism the concept refers

to a fresh start with the 'erasure' and 'rupture' of the existing traditional environment in creating a new urban setting, unleashed from the limiting impositions of the traditional (Kaasa, 2016: 2). Considering the urban history of Turkish Republic, here the concept refers to the generic urban development strategies disengaged from local contexts.

2   In Turkey, the strict precautions and partial lockdowns of COVID-19 lasted for two and a half months, between March 16 and June 1, 2020.

3   *Eyvan* is the main semi-open living area of a traditional house, common in the southeast of Turkey. Opening to an inner courtyard or a terrace on one side, and enclosed by rooms of different functions on the other three, eyvan is also the main circulation space of the house.

References

Akcan, E. (2012) *Architecture in Translation: Germany, Turkey, and the Modern House*. Durham: Duke University Press.

Alioglu, F. (2000) *Mardin Şehir Dokusu ve Evler*. Istanbul: Kent Yayınları.

Batuman, B. (2014) '"Turkey: Modern Architectures in History": Sibel Bozdogan and Esra Akcan Reaktion Books'. *Journal of Architectural Education*, 68(2): 270–1, DOI: 10.1080/10464883.2014.937291

Bozdogan, S. (2001) *Modernism and Nation Building: Turkish Architectural Culture in the Early Republic*. Seattle, WA: University of Washington Press.

Çağlayan, M. (2016) *A modern urbanization on traditional city in the rural of Turkey Republic: the sample of Mardin City*. International Symposium On Civilization, Cities and Architecture, İstanbul.

Cox, C.A. (1998) *Household Interests: Property, Marriage Strategies, and Family Dynamics in Ancient Athens*. Princeton, NJ: Princeton University Press.

Davies, J.K. (1992) 'Society and economy', in D.M. Lewis, J. Boardman, J.K. Davies and M. Ostwald (eds) *The Cambridge Ancient History Volume V: The Fifth Century BC*. Cambridge, UK: Cambridge University Press, pp 287–305.

De Landa, M. (2003) *A Thousand Years of Nonlinear History*. New York: Zone Books.

Kaasa, A. (2016) 'Cohabitation: against the Tabula Rasa and towards a new ethic for cities'. United Nations Habitat III Conference. Retrieved from: www.academia.edu/28623660/Cohabitation_Against_the_Tabula_Rasa_and_Towards_a_New_Ethic_for_Cities

Lefebvre, H. (1996) *Writings on Cities*. Malden, MA: Blackwell.

Tekeli, İ. (2009) 'Türkiye'de Küçük Sermayenin Spekülatif Kentinden Büyük Sermayenin Spekülatif Kentine Bir Geçiş mi Yaşanıyor?', in *Kentsel Arsa, Altyapı ve Kentsel Hizmetler*. İstanbul: Tarih Vakfı Yurt Yayınları, pp 88–93.

Tournikiotis, P. (1999) *The Historiography of Modern Architecture*. Cambridge, MA: The MIT Press.

Tuncer, M. and Aksulu, I. (1993) 'Gap'ta Uygulama Alanlarındaki Tarihsel ve Kentsel Sitlerde Yapı Stoklarının Değerlendirilmesi'. Gap'ta Teknik Hizmetler Sempozyumu, TMMOB, Ankara.

SIX

Towards the Post-Pandemic (Healthy) City: Barcelona's Poblenou Superblock Challenges and Opportunities

Federico Camerin and Luca Maria Francesco Fabris

Introduction

This chapter engages with a specific feature of existing debates about urban design, planning, and COVID-19.[1] We argue that the experience of Superblocks, specifically the case of Barcelona's Poblenou,[2] may succor health, social, and economic inequities and, consequently, may prevent the spread of infectious diseases such as COVID-19. There has not yet been a large public survey to examine the role this new urban design plays in mitigating the effects of COVID-19. Our research therefore sheds important light on the role Superblocks can play in providing a more inclusive, resilient, healthy, sustainable, and safer environment in the context of the COVID-19 pandemic and beyond (see also March and Lehrer; Yerena and Casas, both Volume 3).

After the 2020 pandemic outbreak, a growing number of surveys claimed that environmental factors, such as weather condition and air pollution played a major role in the transmission of the virus (Dobricic et al, 2020; Poirier et al, 2020). Specifically, as shown by Coker et al (2020), long-term exposure to ambient air pollutant concentrations contributes to chronic lung inflammation, a condition that may promote increased severity of COVID-19. In light of these considerations, the pandemic has confronted cities with needing to deal with the high level of congestion and pollution in order to reduce the pandemic's impact on rates of contagion and, consequently, mortality. These issues, along with a lack of community and healthy public spaces (Slater et al, 2020), pose a threat to people's aspirations and experiences of urban living, and have been aggravated by the pandemic outbreak.

As stated by the Organisation for Economic Co-operation and Development (OECD) (2020), cities are implementing policies to reduce private-car use, one of the leading causes of urban air pollution. This has led to an emphasis on slow mobility, shared transportation forms, and providing healthy spaces for urban residents (see Mazumder, Volume 2; Scott, Volume 3; Leanage and Filion, Volume 3; Mayers, Volume 4; Cadena-Gaitán et al, Volume 4). One city that is gradually implementing these kinds of change to overcome the challenges and impacts of COVID-19 is Barcelona. The Spanish city has been working to integrate the COVID-19 recovery with long-term-strategy development updates, using the UN 2030 Agenda of Sustainable Development Goals (SDGs) as a roadmap (Ajuntament de Barcelona, 2020). One of these strategies refers to the concept of Superblocks, which contribute to re-designing the existing built environment. Adopted before COVID-19, the Superblock concept is a measure to lower the World Health Organization recommended air pollution levels, and the frequency and intensity of heat waves due to climate change (López et al, 2020: 7–8).

The concept of Superblock

The Superblock is a social unit, a tight-knit community with shared common facilities, resilient against the stresses of climate change and social vulnerability. It involves the grouping of nine square-shaped blocks of Cerdà's Extension – the late 19th-century planned neighborhoods of Barcelona – resulting in a standardized 400m x 400m urban cell, each with an average of 5,500 inhabitants, including public open spaces, such as streets, sidewalks, and at least one square.[3] This model was conceived in the frame of the so-called 'Ecosystemic Urbanism' principles (Rueda, 2019) through the 2013–18 Urban Mobility Plan of Barcelona by the public consortium BCNEcologia ('Urban Ecology Agency') along with public agreements, initiatives, and strategic tools (that is, 'Citizen Commitment to sustainability – a More Sustainable Barcelona 2012–22'). There are plans for a total of 503 Superblocks across the city.

According to the quantitative health impact assessment by Mueller et al (2020), the Superblock redesign will impact Barcelona's quality of life in a number of key ways. The study estimates that 667 premature deaths per year will be prevented. This is due to a 19.2 percent reduction in private motorized transport, which improves air quality and reduces urban noise. Another factor is the increase in green surfaces from 2.7 m^2/inhabitant to 6.3 m^2/inhabitant in Superblocks in the Extension district area (and up to 7.6 m^2/inhabitant in the Sant Martí district). As a result of this greening, the current heat island effect in a 3x3 block would drop by about -35.9 percent, and public green spaces, including interior patios with blocks and other green surfaces, will increase by 35.8 percent. These changes are expected to create new public spaces on some former roads and to transform some road-crossing into recreational areas, such as picnic tables and space for open-air markets, playgrounds, and sports areas.

As recently stated by Capolongo et al (2020: 16) and Honey-Rosés et al (2020: 8), the application of Superblocks is predicted to have an effect on the negative impacts of COVID-19. The urban cells will help reduce environmental exposure, such as heat, noise, and pollution, while simultaneously increasing physical activity levels and access to green space, thus providing substantial health benefits.

The case study context

The first application of the Superblock concept took place in Poblenou, one Cerdà's Extension neighborhoods, in 2016. It created a 'neighborhood unit' comprised of Badajoz, Pallars, La Llacuna, and Tànger streets (Figure 6.1). Poblenou (a Catalan word meaning 'new village') is located in the north-eastern part of Barcelona. Recognized as a fundamental pillar of Spanish industrialization, the district was part of the stand-alone municipality of Sant Martí dels Provençals until 1897, when it finally joined the municipality of Barcelona. Since the late 1980s, this district has progressively changed its character from a traditional, industrial, lower-middle-class neighbor-hood to an upper-middle-class one. This was due to a series of urban regeneration projects. Currently, this area comprises five neighborhoods belonging to Sant Martí dels Provençals district, for a total population of 91,799 inhabitants and 594,4 ha of surface area. Poblenou's gentrified areas correspond to the large urban projects of 'La Vila Olímpica del Poblenou' (1986–92) and 'Diagonal Mar i el Front Marítim del Poblenou' (1990–2004), which are the 7th and 8th richest neighborhoods in the city, respectively (Ajuntament de Barcelona, 2018: 11). While their income-per-capita index are respectively 164.2 and 150.1 (the medium average index for Barcelona is calculated as 100), 'Provençals del Poblenou' is 22nd (102.3); the Poblenou's Superblock unit is situated in both 'El Parc i la Llacuna del Poblenou' (24th, index 100.4), and 'El Poblenou' (25th, index 99.9). As of January 8, 2021, the area recorded 2,212 cases of COVID-19.[4]

Figure 6.1: Localization of Poblenou's Superblock and neighborhoods and two pictures

Source: F. Camerin (2021)

Poblenou's Superblock implementation: a transformative response to dealing with the challenges of the pandemic?

With an understanding of the potential role that a Superblock can play in mitigating the negative effects of COVID-19, this section examines how changes that have occurred within Poblenou's Superblock are impacting life during the pandemic. Our analysis comprised desk research together with interviews conducted with 15 residents and 15 non-residents, in September 2020.[5]

The renewal of the existing built environment involved the dedication of 13,350m^2 of public spaces to pedestrian use, the doubling of green spaces and tree-lined streets from 9,722m^2 to 18,632m^2, the installation of 349 benches, the reduction of car-parking spaces from 575 to 316, the launching of a growing number of outdoor cultural activities in the new playground areas (2,483m^2), and 37 new premises for activities at street level. These transformations resulted in the opening of 20 new commercial activities within the ground floors of existing buildings (from 65 in 2016 to 85 in 2018). Vehicular traffic rose by 2.6 percent on the four perimeter roads, while the cars circulating within the interior streets dropped by 58 percent. Within these interior streets, there has been an average reduction in daytime noise levels of five decibels (Ajuntament de Barcelona, 2018). In 2020, during the quarantine and the slow reopening, all interviewees positively valued these new urban features of the environment. The reasons given included strengthening the sense of community, security, safety, and well-being, plus the necessity for Barcelona to invest in a public-health-friendly urban design.

As confirmed by our survey conducted in late September 2020, the implementation of Superblocks have helped to mitigate health and socio-economic inequities during the COVID-19 pandemic for a number of reasons. First, the Superblock can produce better air quality, greener environment, and more spaces for slow mobility, which helps to reduce air pollution, noise levels, and heat effects. As shown by Coker et al (2020), long-term exposure to ambient air pollutant concentrations is contributing to chronic lung inflammation, a condition that may promote increased severity of COVID-19. Reducing the population's reliance on cars has been fundamental to enhancing Barcelona's liveability and would address environmental challenges which contribute to lower life expectancy and premature deaths. The measures adopted in Poblenou, such as speed limit restrictions and higher parking costs, reduced the tendency to drive and thereby encouraged the use of bicycles and public transport, thus improving mental and physical health associated with lower levels of pollution and traffic.

Second, the Superblock plays a remarkable role in mitigating the negative effects of density in the post-pandemic environment. There are great advantages to density, particularly from an environmental point of view, through reducing costs, avoiding sprawl, or land waste. However, there could be negative effects from a health point of view, since it makes the lockdown periods more difficult and undermines the possibility of ensuring social distancing. As other chapters in this volume articulate, this is particularly problematic when density intersects with overcrowded living conditions (see Tunstall, Chapter Two; Hubbard, Chapter Four; Kayanan et al, Chapter Seventeen). The Poblenou's Superblock tackled these issues by cutting space for private vehicles, incorporating new walkable spaces with well-connected streets, providing easy access to shops and services, and making public spaces friendlier for residents and city users. By doing so, the Superblock increased the sense of community and the social sustainability, even during the lockdown, by improving the performance, flexibility, and durability of the spaces individuals and families could occupy, while respecting social distancing guidelines.

Third, despite local residents' worries about price increases as a direct result of the improvements introduced in the neighborhood, market values seem to follow the general real estate trends, unaffected by the Superblock-operated change. It has been found that the $€/m^2$ price for second-hand houses for sale in El Parc i la Llacuna del Poblenou neighborhood grew from 3,761 $€/m^2$ of 2016 to 4,144 $€/m^2$ of 2020, thus exceeding the average price of Sant Martí district (from 3,382 $€/m^2$ of 2016 to 3,697 $€/m^2$ of 2020) and the average prices of Barcelona (from 3,478 $€/m^2$ to 4,111 $€/m^2$).[6] Moreover, the new Catalan Law on 'Urgent Measures on Rent Containment in Housing Contracts' of September 2020 will control prices to avoid disproportional increases.[7]

Despite the lack of a public survey on the impact that COVID-19 is having on Poblenou's Superblock, our research shows that residents and non-residents are certain that the basic principles of this model have undoubtedly countered the negative impact of COVID-19 by making these units more inclusive, resilient, sustainable, and safer. Barcelona's Superblock constitutes a valid example of how dense cities can better embody community, wellness, and resilience through redundancy, mix of uses and generations, and decentralization to help residents both satisfying basic needs and living fuller, healthier lives. As demonstrated by the case study, this way to re-design the built environment leads to a reduction in environmental factors that contribute to higher transmission rate of COVID-19, and can help to guarantee the so-called 'right to the city'.

Notes

[1] This work is the result of the strict collaboration between the authors. Sections 3 and 4 are attributed to F. Camerin and sections 1 and 2 to L.M.F. Fabris. Federico Camerin has participated as co-author within the research project 'Former military sites as urban-territorial opportunities in Spain and in Italy: a qualitative classification as an indicator for sustainable and resilient regeneration in postemergency territories', financed by the 'GoforIT' programme of Fondazione CRUI (The Conference of Italian University Rectors) – 2020.

[2] We took into consideration this specific case study as it is the first Superblock unit implemented in Barcelona.

[3] When the Superblock model is applied outside the Cerdà's Extension, the urban cell size changes depending on the existing morphology. The total amount of Superblocks will be 503.

[4] While the most affected neighborhood is 'El Raval', with 3,299 cases.

[5] Statistical reference sample indicated by 'Poblenou Veïns i Veïnes Association'. For more on the data, see the following link: www.researchgate.net/publication/345171344_Interviews_on_ the_implementation_of_Superblock_for_the_edited_book_Global_ Reflections_on_COVID-19_Urban_Inequalities

[6] www.bcn.cat/estadistica/castella/dades/timm/ipreus/hab2mave/evo/
t2mab.htm
[7] http://noticias.juridicas.com/base_datos/CCAA/675381-l-11-2020-de-
18-sep-ca-cataluna-medidas-urgentes-en-materia-de-contencion.html

References

Ajuntament de Barcelona (2018) *Supermanzana del Poblenou*, https://
ajuntament.barcelona.cat/superilles/es/content/poblenou

Ajuntament de Barcelona (2020) *Barcelona nunca se detiene:
plan de acción*, www.barcelona.cat/reactivacioeconomica/es/
plan-de-accion

Capolongo, S., Rebecchi, A., Buffoli, M., Appolloni, L., Signorelli,
C., Fara, G.M. and D'Alessandro, D. (2020) 'COVID-19 and
cities: from urban health strategies to the pandemic challenge.
A decalogue of public health opportunities'. *Acta Bio Medica
Atenei Parmensis*, 91(2): 13–22, DOI: 10.23750/abm.v91i2.9615

Coker, E., Cavalli, L., Fabrizi, E., Guastella, G., Lippo, E., Parisi,
M.L., Pontarollo, N., Rizzati, M., Varacca, A. and Vergalli, S.
(2020) 'The effects of air pollution on COVID-19 related mortality in Northern Italy'. *Environmental and Resource Economics*,
76: 611–34, DOI: 10.1007/s10640-020-00486-1

Dobricic, S., Pisoni, E., Pozzoli, L., Van Dingenen, R., Lettieri, T.,
Wilson, J. and Vignati, E. (2020) *Do environmental factors such as
weather conditions and air pollution influence COVID-19 outbreaks?*
Luxembourg: Publications Office of the European Union,
DOI: 10.2760/6831

Honey-Rosés, J., Anguelovski, I., Chireh, V.K., Daher, C., van den
Bosch, C.K., Litt, J.S., Mawani, V., McCall, M.K., Orellana, A.,
Oscilowicz, E., Sanchez, U., Senbel, M., Tan, X., Villagomez,
E., Zapata, O. and Nieuwenhuijsen, M.J. (2020) 'The impact of
COVID-19 on public space: an early review of the emerging
questions – design, perceptions and inequities'. *Cities & Health*,
1–17, DOI: 10.1080/23748834.2020.1780074

López, I., Ortega, J. and Pardo, M. (2020) 'Mobility infrastructures
in cities and climate change: an analysis through the Superblocks
in Barcelona'. *Atmosphere*, 11: 410.

Mueller, N., Rojas-Rueda, D., Khreis, H. and Cirach, M. (2020) 'Changing the urban design of cities for health: the superblock model'. *Environment International*, 134: 105132.

Organisation for Economic Co-operation and Development (OECD) (2020) *Policy responses to coronavirus (COVID-19): cities policy responses*, www.oecd.org/coronavirus/policy-responses/cities-policy-responses-fd1053ff/

Poirier, C., Luo, W., Majumder, M.S., Liu, D., Mandl, K.D., Mooring, T.A. and Santillana, M. (2020) 'The role of environmental factors on transmission rates of the COVID-19 outbreak: an initial assessment in two spatial scales'. *Scientific Reports*, 10: 17002, DOI: 10.1038/s41598-020-74089-7

Rueda, S. (2019) 'Superblocks for the design of new cities and renovation of existing ones: Barcelona's case', in M. Nieuwenhuijsen and H. Khreis (eds) *Integrating Human Health into Urban and Transport Planning*. New York: Springer, pp 135–53, DOI: 10.1007/978-3-319-74983-9

Slater S.J., Christiana, R.W. and Gustat, J. (2020) 'Recommendations for keeping parks and green space accessible for mental and physical health during COVID-19 and other pandemics'. *Preventing Chronic Disease*, 17: 200204, DOI: 10.5888/pcd17.200204

SEVEN

Urban Crises and COVID-19 in Brazil: Poor People, Victims Again

Wescley Xavier

Introduction

On March 17, 2020, the first death from COVID-19 in Brazil was officially confirmed in Rio de Janeiro. The victim, a 63-year-old domestic worker, contracted COVID-19 from her employer, who had just returned from a trip to Italy. A resident of Miguel Pereira, a small town in the state of Rio de Janeiro, the victim took two buses and a train to cover the 120 km that separated her residence from her workplace, in the Leblon neighborhood, which holds the title of the 'most expensive square meter in the country'. Due to the distance between the two places, the housekeeper 'lived' at her employer's house from Sunday to Thursday. Despite suffering from obesity, diabetes, hypertension, and urinary tract infection, she had to go on working, as she needed the money to help her family.

The first COVID-19 death in Rio de Janeiro is the perfect synthesis of the spread of COVID-19 in Brazil, a country where the virus's lethality is higher among low-income populations, which typically face the more precarious labor, poor housing conditions, and urban mobility problems (see Rocco et al,

Volume 1). Facing the need to keep the Brazilian population at home in the seventh most unequal country in the world, this rich–poor gap proves to be extremely perverse to Black and/or poor populations, particularly those living in Brazilian *favelas*. Considering this context, this chapter aims to explore how the social conditions experienced by Black and/or poor people make the pandemic harsher for these groups.

This chapter is underpinned by the following arguments. First, urban mobility challenges are seriously affecting poor residents on the city's outskirts, as public transportation systems are precarious and insufficient, inducing agglomeration of commuters. Second, the flexibilization of labor laws has aggravated the COVID-19 pandemic as the state has failed to fulfill its mediation role between employer and employee. This places extra pressure on employees to keep working during the pandemic. Third, COVID-19 has been worsened by the state's absence in poor neighborhoods, as noted in *favelas*, where drug dealers and militias formed by police officers control the supply of basic services and mediate commercial transactions. Fourth, the lack of basic sanitation and substandard housing conditions hamper the cleanliness and personal hygiene necessary to avoid the spread of COVID-19. These conditions render social isolation almost impossible, as most residents live in small, overcrowded, and precarious houses in highly populated areas.

Urban mobility and precarious work during the COVID-19 pandemic

In Brazil, urban mobility problems, such as the example that opens this chapter, affect the lives of millions of people, especially those living in large urban areas. Data extracted from the app 'Moovit', based on millions of journeys in 2019, indicate that Brazil has three cities in a top ten list of longest commute time by public transportation in the world. Among them is Rio de Janeiro, which ranks third, with an average travel time of one hour and seven minutes (second only to Istanbul and

Mexico City). This figure considers only the average commute time, whether it is from home to work, or vice-versa. Besides, it should be noted that 11 percent of journeys in Rio de Janeiro take longer than two hours.

Although we used data from Rio de Janeiro as a reference, these patterns are similar in most large Brazilian cities. In addition to the commute time, the situation is aggravated by long waiting times, as users must wait, on average, 19 minutes for their mode of public transportation in the ten largest Brazilian cities. Ultimately, urban mobility is strongly impacted by the increasing precariousness of the mobility modalities, which are heavily concentrated in overcrowded buses.

This phenomenon can be partly explained by an urbanization model that has focused on the spread of cities over larger areas. This model is common in Latin America and the United States and has typically kept the commuter's workplace and residence far apart. Unlike the US, a significant proportion of the Latin American population living on the outskirts and suburbs of large cities cannot afford a car. Therefore, they are heavily dependent on public transportation (Yañez-Pagans et al, 2019).

During the COVID-19 pandemic, this context has contributed to making lower-class Brazilians contagion-prone. Studies conducted by the Federal University of São Paulo (UNIFESP) have shown that deaths from COVID-19 tend to prevail in places where self-employed workers, house-wives, and public transport users predominate. According to the survey, 80 percent of the deaths in the analyzed districts can be explained by the commute percentage of the public transportation system, largely due to the impossibility of social distancing when using such alternatives. On the other hand, when we analyze the data of individuals who use cars as their mode of transport, the effect of this variable on deaths plunges to 39 percent. Furthermore, it is worth mentioning that among the ten districts of the city of São Paulo with the most deaths from COVID-19, nine also rank first in the number of commuters using public transportation.

Similar results were found in the work of Carteni et al (2020), who pointed out the association between Italy's contagion rate and mobility habits, in this case, public transportation, due to the impossibility of social distance. Hadjidemetriou et al (2020) also identified a direct relationship between the increase in case numbers and the use of public transportation in the United Kingdom.

In Brazil, the impact of urban mobility on deaths from COVID-19 is inseparable from precarious work conditions, which have been aggravated by the labor reforms of the administrations of Michel Temer, in 2017, and Jair Bolsonaro, currently underway.[1] Such reforms are characterized by the removal of workers' rights and the reduction of legal mediation of labor relations, where the latter allows the direct negotiation between employer and employee, despite the strong asymmetry inherent in this relationship.

The effects of weaker labor laws were noted as early as the first year after the Labor Reform when the number of lawsuits in the labor court dropped by 36 percent in 2018. Two of the alleged arguments to support the reform were the reduction of informality, which reached 40.8 percent in 2017, according to the Instituto Brasileiro de Geografia e Estatística (IBGE) (2018b), and the potential increase in the employment rate. However, the formal employment rate has remained largely intact, while informal jobs have increased by 5.5 percent. It is precisely the combination of informal work with poor mobility conditions that increases the spread of COVID-19 among the poorest population, who are unable to stay home and are exposed on overcrowded buses and trains.

In response to the crisis and under pressure from the National Congress, in April 2020, the Brazilian government created the Emergency Program for the Maintenance of Employment and Income.[2] The program grants a monthly payment of BRL 600 – approximately USD 112 – to informal workers and individuals enrolled in the Federal Government's Single Registry for social programs. Despite the relevance of the measures, the absence of regulation that guarantees jobs in the post-pandemic scenario is perceived as an aggravation to informality.

Housing and sanitary conditions as antecedents of contagion and death from COVID-19

The precarious working conditions of millions of Brazilians must be perceived as antecedents to several other social problems, among which we highlight the poor and unsanitary living conditions of a significant share of the population. As previously mentioned, the scattered formation of Brazilian urban areas has confined residents to peripheral areas far from their workplaces and many essential services. Additionally, these services are aggravated by the rugged topography and the historic occupation of hillside areas, such as in Rio de Janeiro, resulting in densely populated communities commonly known as *favelas*.

The Brazilian *favelas* are home to 13.6 million residents, implying a high population density. While the city of Rio de Janeiro has a population density of 5,556 inhabitants/km^2, its largest *favela*, called Rocinha, has 48,258 inhabitants/km^2 (Data. Rio, 2020). Besides the class relations, there are also disparities which put Black people at greater risk than White people. In Rio's favelas, 66 percent of habitants are Black (Berenguer, 2014), which contrasts with the racial profile of the city as a whole, which is 50 percent Black or mixed-race, and differs strongly with South Zone neighborhoods, where 80 percent of residents are White (Rio On Watch, 2015).

The density described here concerns both the concentration of houses in a single neighborhood (density) and the number of people per dwelling (overcrowding). This combination makes social distancing or isolation impossible, not only because the limited space and overcrowding within dwellings brings people closer, but it also makes the street a key leisure space, especially for children (see Rocco et al, Volume 1). This, in turn, increases the chances of spreading viruses causing acute respiratory diseases, such as COVID-19 (Góes et al, 2019).

In addition to urban density and overcrowding, another factor resulting from the absence of the state makes the poorest areas of Brazilian cities more susceptible to COVID-19 infection. We must add the omission of public authorities in the provision of minimal infrastructure, which leads to the poor sanitary conditions imposed on residents of *favelas* and other lower-class neighborhoods. According to the World Bank (2018), Brazil invested about 2 percent of its GDP in infrastructure, which is a much lower percentage compared to countries with similar characteristics (Costa, 2020).

Among the key recommendations of the World Health Organization to reduce the transmission of COVID-19 are social isolation and simple hygiene habits, such as washing our hands with soap. Nonetheless, many residents of poor areas of Brazil are unable to follow the latter, as they do not have access to clean water or sewage services (see Lemanski and De Groot, Volume 1). The percentage of households with access to clean water is lower in the North and Northeast regions of Brazil. For instance, in 2019, only 49.5 percent of households in the state of Pará had access to clean water. When we analyze data from Belém, the state capital, this percentage increases to 75.2 percent (Rodrigues, 2020).

However, this scenario is not restricted to the North and Northeast regions. In general, sanitation conditions put Brazil at risk, as 14.2 percent of the population does not have access to clean water, while 33.7 percent of the population lives in areas without sanitation (IBGE, 2018a). In many residences, especially in urban agglomerations formed by occupations, as is the case in many *favelas*, the poor design and execution of the houses limit the installation of water tanks. Besides, water and sanitation companies demand documentation to prove ownership of the land to provide services, which is rather unusual in the illegally occupied settlements.

In this way, poor housing and sanitary conditions increase the spread of COVID-19 because they do not allow the social isolation of infected individuals, due to the number of residents per home and the proximity between residencies – aggravated by the pressure of parallel power in keeping the *favelas* functioning during the pandemic. Poor water and sewage infrastructure conditions make the scenario even more critical, preventing basic hygienic care.

Conclusion

The purpose of this chapter was to shed light on elements that make COVID-19 a much more lethal disease for poor populations living in unhealthy housing conditions. The main arguments presented here refer to the conditions that preceded the pandemic, all of which derived from the absence or omission of the state, such as poor housing conditions and basic services, urban mobility, and the flexibilization of labor laws, which lead to underemployment (see also Stevens, Chapter Eight).

The consequences are extremely damaging to the population living on the outskirts of Brazilian cities. Amid inequality, COVID-19 hits Black and poor populations harder. Indeed, according to data from the Center for Operations and Health Intelligence (NOIS) at PUC-Rio (2020), these groups are four times more likely to die from COVID-19 when compared to the White middle-class population. In short, the context outlined in this chapter indicates that, in times of discourse for the minimal state around the world, the COVID-19 pandemic shows once again that the absence of public power is the *causa mortis* of part of the population.

Notes

[1] The Labor Reform, enacted by then-President Michel Temer in 2017, aimed to simplify labor relations and thereby increase the number of jobs. With the new labor laws, the rules that were historically mediated by unions are now defined by employees and employers, such as the definition of work hours, rest time, vacation time, and salary negotiations. These reforms have been criticized because they tend to accelerate the

precariousness of work by releasing companies from a series of previously existing worker rights, and because it is understood that negotiations involving the worker and the employer are totally asymmetrical.

[2] The Emergency Program for the Maintenance of Employment and Income was instituted in April 2020 by the Federal Government. The purpose of the program was to guarantee income to workers who had their work hours reduced or work contracts interrupted by their employers and to relieve companies that suspended their economic activities during the pandemic. The suspension of the work contract, partial or total, could be done by the employer for up to 60 days, and it was mandatory for companies that joined the program to guarantee employees' jobs for a period proportional to the benefits that were paid by the Federal Government.

References

Berenguer, L.O. (2014) 'The favelas of Rio de Janeiro: a study of sico-spatial segregation and racial discrimination'. *Revista Iberoamericana de Estudios de Desarollo*, 3: 104–34, https://doi.org/10.26754/ojs_ried/ijds.87

Carteni, A., Di Francesco, L. and Martino, M. (2020) 'How mobility habits influenced the spread of the COVID-19 pandemic: results from the Italian case study'. *Science of the Total Environment*, 741: 1–9, https://doi.org/10.1016/j.scitotenv.2020.140489

Costa, S.S. (2020) 'The pandemic and the labour market in Brazil'. *Revista de Administração Pública*, 54(4): 969–78, http://dx.doi.org/10.1590/0034-761220200170

Data.Rio (2020) *Rio em Síntese: população e domicílio*. Retrieved from: www.data.rio/pages/rio-em-sntese-2

Góes, L.G.B., Zerbinati, R.M., Tateno, A.F., Souza, A.V., Ebach, F., Corman, V.M., Moreira-Filho, C.A., Durigon, E.L., Silva-Filho, L.V.R.F. and Drexler, J.F. (2019) 'Typical epidemiology of respiratory virus infections in a Brazilian slum'. *Journal of Medical Virology*, 92: 1316–21, http://dx.doi.org/10.1002/jmv.25636

Hadjidemetriou, G.M., Sasidharan, M., Kouyialis, G. and Parlikad, A.K. (2020) 'The impact of government measures and human mobility trend on COVID-19 related deaths in the UK'. *Transportation Research Interdisciplinary Perspectives*, 6: 1–6, https://doi.org/10.1016/j.trip.2020.100167

Instituto Brasileiro de Geografia e Estatística (IBGE) (2018a) *Pesquisa Nacional por Amostra de Domicílios Contínua*. Retrieved from: https://biblioteca.ibge.gov.br/visualizacao/livros/liv101654_informativo.pdf

Instituto Brasileiro de Geografia e Estatística (IBGE) (2018b) 'Síntese de indicadores sociais: uma análise das condições de vida da população brasileira'. *Estudos e Pesquisas. Informação Demográfica e Socioeconômica*, 39. Retrieved from: https://biblioteca.ibge.gov.br/visualizacao/livros/liv101629.pdf

NOIS PUC-Rio (2020) *Análise socioeconômica da taxa de letalidade da Covid-19 no Brasil*. Retrieved from: https://drive.google.com/file/d/1tSU7mV4OPnLRFMMY47JIXZgzkklvkydO/view

Rio On Watch (2015) *Maps show racial segregation in Rio de Janeiro*. Retrieved from: www.rioonwatch.org/?p=25311

Rodrigues, R.I. (2020) *Nota Técnica: a Covid-19, a falta de água nas favelas e o direito à moradia no Brasil*. Brasília: IPEA. Retrieved from: http://repositorio.ipea.gov.br/bitstream/11058/10109/1/NT_39_Diest_A%20Covid_19%20a%20falta%20de%20agua%20nas%20favelas.pdf

World Bank (2018) *Public policy notes – towards a fair adjustment and inclusive growth*. Retrieved from: www.worldbank.org/en/country/brazil/brief/brazil-policy-notes

Yañez-Pagans, M.D., Mitnik, O.A., Scholl, L. and Vazquez, A. (2019) 'Urban transport systems in Latin America and the Caribbean: lessons and challenges'. *Latin American Economic Review*, 28(1): 1–25, https://doi.org/10.1186/s40503-019-0079-z

EIGHT

Flexible Temporalities, Flexible Trajectories: Montreal's Nursing Home Crisis as an Example of Temporary Workers' Complicated Urban Labor Geographies

Lukas Stevens

On April 11, 2020 the Premier of Quebec, François Legault, confirmed 31 residents of the long-term care facility Maison Herron located in a Montreal suburb had died of complications related to infections with the COVID-19 virus. Montreal was already the epicenter of the Canadian pandemic, yet the circumstances of these deaths – care workers had effectively abandoned the facility for fear of contracting the virus due to unsafe working conditions – shed light on the dire situation in both public and private care homes known by their French acronym CHSLD (centres d'hébergement de soins de longue durée). By July 2020, nearly 70 percent of the COVID-19-related deaths in Quebec (most of which were in the Montreal metropolitan area) occurred in such facilities, and they routinely lost up to 40 percent of residents to the virus (Carman, 2020).

Concurrently, disadvantaged urban boroughs such Montreal-Nord or Mercier–Hochelaga-Maisonneuve emerged as community hotspots. Although yet to be empirically proven, early assessments by public health experts link both the spread of the virus between Montreal care homes and within the community to the high concentration of low-income health care workers, who live in these dense boroughs and work in multiple homes (Santé Montréal, 2020). Care work requires prolonged physical contact with patients, thereby creating the conditions for workers to contract COVID-19, carry it to other care homes, and infect their own families. However, unions and scholars more explicitly blame the historically poor working conditions in Quebec's CHSLD system, which predate the pandemic, as the main cause for uncontrolled transmission: low wages and short-term contracts force workers to seek out jobs at several understaffed facilities – often mediated by temporary staffing agencies who take a percentage of the wage. Care work thus is 'one of the most precarious jobs in Quebec', according to Quebecois labor scholar François Aubry (Monpetit, 2020).

In this chapter I outline how the spread of COVID-19 in Montreal care homes not only made the poor working conditions within CHSLDs public, but also reveals important, yet previously invisible, information about the complex and precarious geographies low-income health care workers servicing multiple care homes encounter daily. These involve long and irregular commutes likely occurring across the entire metropolitan area (for international examples, see Xavier, Chapter Seven; Rocco et al, Volume 1; Sternberg, Volume 1). While the data presented in this study is preliminary and specific to Montreal, it is consistent with previous discussions on the labor geography of low-wage workers whose employment is mediated by staffing agencies (Peck and Theodore, 2001; Enright, 2013). This case study thus functions as an example of how the COVID-19 crisis can be used to reimagine data collection on employment geographies, in particular for low-wage jobs with difficult to predict spatial patterns.

The urban geographies of mediated labor

Mediated labor – a contractual triangulation between the worker, their agency, and the client purchasing their labor – is a common fixture in most labor markets in the Global North and routinely makes up to 2 percent of national work forces (Coe et al, 2010). Next to manual labor, agency mediated work is common among personal care services such as childcare or eldercare in Canada (Fudge and Strauss, 2014), thus allowing Montreal's CHSLD workers to function as a case study of how COVID-19 highlights the industry's complex geographies. Temporary work is also a decidedly urban arrangement, yet few attempts have been made to trace the intra-metropolitan geographies of staffers – their daily trajectories and the distribution of work locations throughout metropolitan areas – within North American cities to the same degree as has been done with higher-wage workers (Peck and Theodore, 2001; Enright, 2013, Ojala and Pyöriä, 2018).

However, consistencies emerge. Studies on metropolitan geographies conclude that staffing agencies determine the location of their recruitment office primarily through access to potential future workers. As mediated labor is mainly employed in the low-wage segment of the labor market, agencies tend to agglomerate around 'sources' of low wage labor such as welfare offices or low-income neighborhoods (Peck and Theodore, 2001; Cranford and Vosko, 2006).

The location of the agencies and neighborhoods from which workers are recruited appears to have little influence over the geographic area serviced, that is, where client firms and organizations, such as Montreal's CHSLDs, are located. Temporary staffers therefore travel extensively and flexibly. In a Canadian example, Cranford and Vosko (2006) note that client firms tend to be dispersed throughout the Toronto metropolitan area, thereby creating complicated trajectories for staffers, which can be concurrent (multiple work sites throughout the day) or consecutive (changing work locations every several days, weeks or months).

The practice of recruiting staffers from low-income neighborhoods further complicates the labor geographies of workers. Whereas higher-wage workers with stable employment locations are able to choose a residential area to optimize their commute, high levels of pre-existing precarity among residents of low-income neighborhoods prevent workers from having such choice (Enright, 2013). The workers most mobile and reliant on public transit connections are therefore among the population with the least access to such services.

Although consistent geographic patterns have been observed in multiple qualitative case studies on urban temporary staffing, the collection of representative data remains challenging. First, national and regional data collection strategies such as the census or origin-destination data, which are commonly used in economic geography to identify spatial employment patterns, provide a narrow picture of where labor is performed (see Shearmur et al, Volume 4). Second, such data do not capture changes to employment location throughout the year as census data are designed to provide a snapshot of the moment during which they are collected. Third, employment agencies frequently function on the periphery of the labor law, thus making it notoriously difficult to collect accurate data (Enright, 2013; Fudge and Strauss, 2014). For these reasons it is important to consider alternative forms of data collection to capture the trajectories and work locations of mediated labor. The sudden changes to labor geographies instigated by COVID-19-related lockdowns present opportunities to find such alternatives.

The labor geographies of Montreal's care workers

This analysis is based on data on the number of COVID-19 infections in both care homes and boroughs within the Montreal metropolitan region. The data were collected and published by the provincial public health department – Institut national de santé publique du Québec (INSPQ) (2020) – and metropolitan equivalent, Santé Montréal, on a daily basis. Although the peak infection rate in care homes during the first wave of the pandemic occurred in late April 2020, the CHSLD data used in this chapter are from April 15, 2020 – the week the full extent of the crisis became public.

Figure 8.1 maps the locations of long-term care homes in the Montreal metropolitan region in which more than 15 percent of the residence had contracted COVID-19 on April 15, 2020. Low-income neighborhoods in which community transmission was highest and where many CHSLD care workers live are

Figure 8.1: The location of infected CHSLD homes

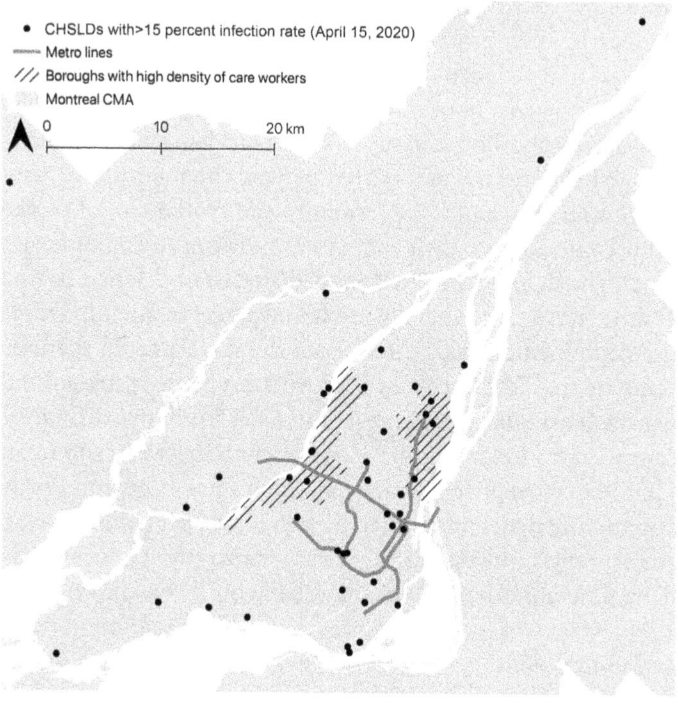

Source: map created by author, using data from INSPQ, 2020; Santé Montréal, 2020

also highlighted. The Montreal metro system, which services the City of Montreal as well as suburban communities to the north and south of the Montreal Island, is included in the map to provide a scale reference and to discuss the complex trajectories the analysis implies.

Some important geographic patterns emerge from this simple mapping. Although there are centrally located CHSLDs, many care homes are located in close proximity to the Saint Lawrence river, in whose midst the Island of Montreal is located. These parts of the Montreal region are generally suburban or even peri-urban in character and thus have limited public transit connectivity. In contrast, the boroughs in which community transition was the highest and in which public health officials estimate the highest concentration of low-income care workers reside are found on the periphery of Montreal's center, as can be seen by their proximity to the city's urban metro network.

Rose and Twigge-Molecey (2013) note that Montreal's low-income neighborhoods are better served by transit than similar neighborhoods in most other Canadian cities. Yet many affected care homes are located beyond the metro lines, thus suggesting that transit use requires care workers to also take suburban buses for their commutes between their home and employment location. Further, mediated labor practices as well as short-term gigs generally result in workers frequenting multiple employment sites throughout the day. As temp agencies tend to mediate workers within the entire metropolitan region (Peck and Theodore, 2001), it is likely that Montreal care workers frequently have to commute between suburban CHSLDs during their work day. Such inter-suburban cross-commuting defies the primary design intentions behind North American transit systems, which prioritize trips between residential neighborhoods and the urban core (Anas and Arnott, 1998). Care workers' trajectories are therefore time-consuming and unreliable.

It is important to note that this analysis is preliminary: while health officials have established that the spread of COVID-19 within low-income neighborhoods as well as the CHSLD system was aided by the high density of mobile care workers, definite claims about their labor geographies cannot be made without supplementary data. It would be premature to conclude that the apparent commutes are indeed accurate as the residential neighborhoods individual care workers live in, the amount of work locations each frequents, or how often these work locations change remain speculative. In particular, it is difficult to assert whether care workers do service the entire metropolitan area or whether their work is regionalized, that is, that care workers living in northern boroughs primarily service northern CHSLDs. The location of agencies recruiting care workers is also unclear. Nonetheless, the rapid spread of COVID-19 between care homes does suggest widespread cross-commuting between suburban locations. Furthermore, recent reforms to the care system have explicitly specified that CHSLD personnel are interchangeable across amalgamated health care areas (Sampson, 2020): both labor unions and health researchers have repeatedly explained that new 'lean' management methods, relying on temporary and mobile workers, pose threats to the health of care givers and receivers (Goudreau and Soares, 2019). The devastating effects of COVID-19 for CHSLD residents and workers confirms their warnings were warranted.

Conclusion

The decentralized geographies of mediated labor in metropolitan areas are generally understudied. This is partially by design and partially due to the inability of current governmental data collection strategies to accurately capture the flexible labor trajectories. As COVID-19 has revealed, however, the location of where labor can be performed and the control workers have over that location are determined by workplace status, and, in the case of care workers in Quebec, by provincial directives. In urban settings, the most mobile workers thus are often those with the least workplace power.

The case study provided in this chapter is specific to the spread of COVID-19 in Montreal and the province of Quebec. Further, care labor may not be a profession in which mediated labor is common in other North American contexts as temporary staffing markets are highly localized (Enright, 2013). However, this case still provides important lessons about labor geographies of mediated employment, which are consistent with previous studies. First, it reveals how the trajectories of workers whose employment is mediated by a staffing agency are flexible, unpredictable, and counter the design intentions of North American transportation systems. Second, it demonstrates how the COVID-19 pandemic provides opportunities to observe patterns of unequal labor geographies found in North American cities. However, these patterns are neither novel nor a momentary result of the pandemic. They have simply been brought into clearer view, thereby highlighting the importance of paying further attention to the complex and detrimental intra-metropolitan labor trajectories of low-wage workers.

References

Anas, A. and Arnott, R. (1998) 'Urban spatial structure'. *Journal of Economic Literature*, 36(3): 1426–64.

Carman, T. (2020) 'Canada's hardest-hit nursing homes lost 40% of residents in just 3 months of the pandemic'. CBC. Retrieved from: www.cbc.ca/news/canada/nursing-home-COVID-19-deaths-1.5641266

Coe, N.M., Jones, K. and Ward, K. (2010) 'The business of temporary staffing: a developing research agenda'. *Geography Compass*, 4(8): 1055–68.

Cranford, C. and Vosko, L. (2006) 'Conceptualizing precarious employment mapping wage work across social location and occupational context', in L. Vosko (ed) *Precarious Employment: Understanding Labour Market Insecurity in Canada*. Montreal: McGill-Queens University Press.

Enright, B. (2013) '(Re)considering new agents: a review of labour market intermediaries within labour geography'. *Geography Compass*, 7(4): 287–99.

Fudge, J. and Strauss, K. (2014) *Temporary Work, Agencies and Unfree Labour: Insecurity in the New World of Work*. Abingdon: Routledge, Taylor & Francis Group.

Goudreau, M. and Soares, A. (2019) 'Approche "industrielle" dans le réseau de la santé: une enquête publique s'impose'. *La Presse*, December 5. Retrieved from: www.lapresse.ca/debats/opinions/2019-12-05/approche-industrielle-dans-le-reseau-de-la-sante-une-enquete-publique-s-impose

Institut national de santé publique du Québec (INSPQ) (2020) 'État de situation des cas confirmés et des décès par CHSLD en date du 15 avril 2020'. Retrieved from: www.scribd.com/document/456629085/List-of-CHSLDs-in-Quebec-with-COVID-19-cases

Montpetit, J. (2020) 'Why are Quebec's nursing homes so understaffed, and what's being done about it?' CBC, April 15. Retrieved from: www.cbc.ca/news/canada/montreal/quebec-nursing-homes-understaffed-1.5531997

Ojala, S. and Pyöriä, P. (2018) 'Mobile knowledge workers and traditional mobile workers: assessing the prevalence of multi-locational work in Europe'. *Acta Sociologica*, 61(4): 402–18.

Peck, J. and Theodore, N. (2001) 'Contingent Chicago: restructuring the spaces of temporary labor'. *International Journal of Urban and Regional Research*, 25(3): 471–96.

Rose, D. and Twigge-Molecey, A. (2013) *A city-region growing apart? Taking stock of income disparity in greater Montreal, 1970–2005*. Research Paper No. 222, Cities Centre, Toronto, ON: University of Toronto.

Sampson, X. (2020) 'Crise dans les CHSLD: une succession de réformes malavisées'. Retrieved from: https://ici.radio-canada.ca/nouvelle/1700150/reforme-sante-barrette-couillard-consequences-structure-covid

Santé Montréal (2020) 'État de Situation Montreal Arrondissements' [Report]. Retrieved from: www.cbc.ca/news/canada/montreal/montreal-low-income-inequality-COVID-19-1.5570296

PART II

Experiences of Housing and Home During the Pandemic

NINE

Bold Words, a Hero or a Traitor? Fang Fang's Diaries of the Wuhan Lockdown on Chinese Social Media

Liangni Sally Liu, Guanyu Jason Ran, and Yu Wang

Introduction

The central Chinese city of Wuhan was the initial epicenter of the COVID-19 pandemic and the first city to experience lockdown. The 11 million residents of Wuhan were locked down for 76 consecutive days, beginning in late January 2020. Fang Fang, a well-known Chinese writer as well as a resident of the city, published her personal accounts of the lockdown experience in the form of diaries on Weibo and WeChat, two of the most popular Chinese social media platforms. At the beginning, the diaries were well-received by Chinese netizens because of their bold critique of social injustice, corruption, abuse of power, and other sensitive issues in China that deterred the efficient government response to the pandemic. However, soon after the diaries were translated into English and German and published with a fast-track process overseas, Chinese public attitudes towards the diaries drastically swung against it. Many initial supporters turned to express their concerns and suspicions of the publication's intention. The prevailing opinion was that the writing sabotaged China's efforts to fight the pandemic and fed into conspiracy theories and wider anti-China political sentiment. The author was criticized as an opportunist and traitor who capitalized on the health crisis to enhance her own credentials. In Chinese social media, a polarized reception of the diaries emerged.

This chapter explores how the diaries have provided a rare discursive site for the Chinese public to engage in political deliberations and ideological debate about democratic liberalism and populist patriotism which co-exist in contemporary China. Empirical data include some key commentary articles[1] about the diaries from both sides of arguments that circulated on WeChat and the responses these articles attracted. The chapter also explores some of the lived experiences during lockdown, as described in Fang Fang's diaries.

About the diaries

Even before the diaries caught the public's attention, Fang Fang was a respected novelist of realist fiction and was well known in Chinese literary circles since the 1980s. Her writing sympathetically portrays difficult experiences of ordinary people in China. From January 25 to March 24, 2020, Fang Fang posted 60 diaries on both Weibo and WeChat, written in colloquial language. Even though these original posts were constantly censored, many Chinese netizens helped to repost and circulate them on various social media platforms. This is why these diaries survived intact from Chinese censorship restrictions. The diaries can be broadly grouped into five thematic categories: 1) the author's personal and daily life and experience under the lockdown, including grocery shopping, housework, transportation, family relations, and online communication with family members and friends; 2) the author's reception of information from family members, friends, and colleagues; 3) her emotional reactions to many pandemic-related realities;

4) her critique about the government's belated reporting on COVID-19 to the public and bureaucratic system and corruption that deterred the efficient government response to the pandemic; and 5) the author's reflection on some long-standing issues of social inequalities, including urban inequalities, which, like elsewhere, were familiar to ordinary Chinese people but became highlighted in the context of the health crisis.

The following excerpts from her diaries provide a better picture of how Fang Fang described the lockdown. She recorded her dairy life and experiences, which mirrored the apocalyptic sights the pandemic-related lockdown brought to a city. For example, she detailed how she picked up her daughter from the airport: 'There were hardly any cars or pedestrians on the street. Those few days were when panic and fright were at their height in the city. We both wore facemasks'.[2] She described how neighbors cooperated with each other to collect food from grocery shops while social distancing: 'When the food arrives, we lower buckets from our apartment windows and reel it up, as if it were minnows in a net'. She portrayed the empty city as 'quiet and beautiful, almost majestic', and the empty East Lake of the city like the 'deserted and peaceful expanse of the water, but this virus continues to roam the city like an evil spirit, appearing whenever and wherever it pleases'. Such descriptions of despair were also echoed by her mourning of the virus as a public trauma, and how the outbreak impacted people's mental well-being: 'We all felt completely helpless in the face of these patients crying out, desperate for help'. In her writing, the fear, terror, frustration, anger, anxiety, and boredom related to the lockdown are all described in detail; Fang Fang called for 'an army of councillors to help people through the aftermath'.

As the diaries began to attract more attention online, Fang Fang started to incorporate information gleaned from text messages and phone calls from her family members and well-connected friends who were working in medical fields, forming a written collage of Wuhan. For example, she mentioned what her brother (a lecturer at Huazhong University of Science and Technology) warned her about how deadly the virus could be: 'On December 31, he forwarded to me an essay entitled "Suspected case of virus of unknown origin in Wuhan"'. In another diary entry, she wrote: 'A doctor friend said to me: "In fact, we doctors have all known for a while that there is a human-to-human transmission of the disease, we reported this to our superiors, but yet nobody warned people"'. Overall, she kept tabs on what was happening outside her apartment in these diaries as well.

At another point, Fang Fang used the diaries to tackle some broader social and political problems that unfolded during the lockdown. Her critiques are multi-layered, starting to question the efficiency of the public health system, and to tell the truth that the collapsed public system had resulted in public devastation. For instance, she wrote: 'Hospital system was brought to the brink of collapse' and 'The infected ended up traipsing all over the city, in the wind and rain, searching in vain for treatment'. These discourses were further developed into the condemnation of the officialdom and formalism in the early stages of the local government's handling of the outbreak: 'The political party leaders here in Wuhan have requested that the citizens provide a public expression of gratitude toward the Chinese Communist Party'. By criticizing the dysfunction of the local government in the pandemic, Fang Fang eventually pointed out: 'Governments are servants of the people, not the other way round', and demanded answers from the government:

> We now have to pay for the disastrous consequences from the ban on speaking the truth, the prevention of the media from reporting the true facts. Who was responsible for delay, procrastination and disinformation? What kind of human failure made the two months lockdown of a province of 60 million people necessary?

Fang Fang's battles with the Chinese censors are a significant part of the narrative: 'posts get deleted, then reposted, over and over again … Once things get to this point, I have to ask my dear internet censors, do you think you can really delete it all?' She also expressed her frustration about the lack of transparency of information: 'You won't even give us a clear answer as to when it will end so we can at least have a target in mind'.

Urban inequalities are also a part of her narrative, especially in her writing about economically and socially disadvantageous people and their inability to access medical treatments in hospitals. For example, in one diary entry in February 2020, Fang Fang wrote:

> As predicted, we are seeing a spike of cases now. Some of those infected but cannot get into the hospital are at the end of their tether. Someone jumped from a bridge last night. A community worker told us a whole family had been infected but cannot get into the hospital. One has died. In desperation, the rest want to end their lives.

Wrapping up all observations and critiques, advocating for social justice becomes the central theme of the diaries:

> What really needs to be said is that the true test of a country's level of civility has nothing to do with building the tallest skyscraper or driving the fastest car, nor does it matter how advanced your military might be; it is also not about how advanced your technology is or even your artistic achievement. There is only one test, and that is how you treat the weakest and most vulnerable members of your society.

As can be seen, the diaries tell the story of the virus at ground level and chronicle the experiences of the first lockdown of the first outbreaks of COVID-19. They are an entirely human portrait of life and experience under this extraordinary circumstance. They document lived experiences and capture some significant moments of this global pandemic. More importantly, the diaries reveal some systematic issues of mainland Chinese society which impeded the response to the pandemic from the very beginning.

A polarized reception of the diaries in Chinese social media

More importantly, the diaries served as an alternative and crucial source of information for many Chinese during a chaotic time. This was a time when information about the contagious virus was in high demand, but was tightly controlled and heavily filtered by state media in China. This is one reason that the diaries attracted many supporters on Chinese social media, as one commentary article describes:

> The diaries are a presentation of what people suffered in Wuhan. The writing has some flaws, but it at least records the reality. It is much more reliable than some [Chinese] mainstream media reports, telling people that the virus is not transmitted from person to person.[3]

Support for the diaries also came from many well-educated Chinese people from intellectual backgrounds, who were pro-freedom of speech and advocated social responsibility and work ethics as righteous writers. One commentary article took a strong standpoint in favor of the diaries by saying: 'I believe that Fang Fang is a lonely but brave soul because she refused to adopt the standard government narrative of recording the lockdown. I want to say you are not alone'.[4] Another commentator praised Fang Fang because she offered: 'a rare luxury thing in China – that is truth'.[5] Later, when Fang Fang was heavily criticized and resentment towards her stirred up on Chinese social media, some commentary articles supported her by pointing out that the accusation towards Fang Fang and how her writing was received by the public was just like the political persecution enforced by Chairman Mao towards intellectual people during China's Cultural Revolution in the 1960s and 1970s.[6]

In general, the diaries were initially well received on Chinese social media. Fang Fang became a national hero who spoke the truth and held government agencies who mishandled the initial phase of the outbreak and suppressed information, to account. However, soon after the publisher, HarperCollins, announced that the diaries would be translated into English and published under the title *Wuhan Diary: Dispatches from a Quarantined City*, Fang Fang started to suffer heavy nationalist backlash online. Even many of her previous supporters turned against her. The arguments opposing Fang Fang and her diaries were multi-dimensional and centered on several issues. The first was that many people suggested that the information presented in the diaries was not entirely truthful. For example, one article said: 'There was never a first-hand information source. The narrative often used in the diaries is "I heard from …" or "One of my doctor friends told me …". If the information was heard from others, does it mean it is not entirely true?'[7] The most controversial issue was about a description in the diaries that a large pile of cell phones was left on the ground at a funeral home crematorium, with nobody claiming them. This text was paired with a picture of the cell phones on the ground, which implied how many people died during the pandemic without family members present, and how cruelly the dying were treated. Subsequently, it was determined that this account was not true, and was, instead, based on rumors circulating at the time. The same was also true for a diary account of the tragic death of a nurse, who died without anyone present.

The second argument was centered on concerns about the negativity and darkness the diaries exerted during a time when positivity and encouragement were mostly needed.

One article expressed: 'When people in the frontline were fighting hard, Fang Fang hid herself in the house to use her pen as a weapon to undermine all effort other people made to contain the virus'.[8]

The third argument against the diaries concerned how they would impact China's image and position on the international stage, especially at the time when the US and China were in the midst of a diplomatic conflict (BBC News, 2020). One commentary article discussed how as the virus continued to spread around the world and people started to become more critical of China's response to the outbreak, any heavy scrutiny or criticism might result in an accentuation of the blame on China. At a certain point, the article said: 'A translated version of Fang's critical account of the Wuhan outbreak would only provide opponents of China with more ammunition'.[9] Because of these factors, opinions towards Fang Fang quickly changed from truth-telling hero to a traitor to her home country. One response to the article said: 'She was capitalising on her fame – and even possibly a tragedy. She is seizing this time of national crisis and taking advantage [of it]. This is contemptible'.[10]

It is well known that Chinese cyber-nationalism is a growing phenomenon and promoted by many nationalistic Chinese netizens. They use internet resources to exert their nationalist ideas and to promote the Chinese government's political propaganda (Ying, 2012). Fang Fang's critiques of the Chinese government cause many Chinese netizens to accuse the English-language published diaries of 'hand[ing] over the knife to anti-Chinese sentiment and provide legitimacy to conspiracy theories and unjustified blame on China' (Xia, 2020). It is worth pointing out that for many Chinese netizens, the timing of the foreign-language publications of the diaries was tricky. At that time, the virus was continuing to spread around the world. Political leaders in some countries were blaming China for the pandemic, and therefore anything that stigmatized China could result in Chinese patriotic netizens' aggressive online behavior in order to defend their own country. A common phrase used in such a case is: '*Shuai Guo (甩锅)*' which means using somebody else as a scapegoat. Many Chinese commentary articles adopted this phrase as a metaphor to support their argument that, in fact, some Western governments tried to shift public focus and condemnation towards China, in order to cover up their own mishandlings of the pandemic. The Trump administration was one of the most prominent examples of a country that used this strategy, and they spared no effort to blame China for allowing the virus to seep into the world at large.

Conclusion: political deliberation versus ideological debate

Overall, the controversy around the diaries caused a clash in Chinese society between different groups of people who possess divergent political ideologies, just like one commentary article mentioned: 'This [controversy] is a societal split caused by the diaries ... the translated version of the diaries published overseas has resulted in a national war of words'.[11] As illustrated earlier, the diaries are critical of Chinese governance during the onset of the pandemic, especially local governance. The contention about the diaries among netizens on Chinese social media reflects the diverse political points of view of Chinese people, which are rarely presented in the Western world; namely, some support the Chinese communist regime and populist patriotism, while others are against autocracy but pro democratic liberalism and civil participation in governance. One general perception about China is that the Chinese politics is monochromatic (Wasserstrom, 2008; Chen, 2010); however, the controversy about the diaries tells the opposite: that diverse political deliberations strongly exists even under a totalitarian political regime, and critical social events, such as a pandemic outbreak, normally plays a vital role in stimulating the outward expression of these deliberations. Health crises can often catalyze existing social and political tension of a society (Woods et al, 2020). This has been demonstrated in the case of China during the COVID-19 pandemic.

Moreover, the reluctance to face critical commentaries that were presented in the diaries also reflects broader underlying anxieties that many Chinese nationals have towards China's international reputations. Regardless of the economic power of China today, many Chinese nationals are also aware of the problematic aspect of Chinese governance and its implications to societal developments. They understand that China's further development is not only determined by its economic power but also upon its image in the international political arena, relations with other important countries, and its positioning within the existing world order and global context. As a result, many Chinese nationals are particularly cautious about how China is portrayed; accordingly, they have become defenders of China's international reputation when necessary.

The contention of Fang Fang's diaries sheds further light on the development of nationalism in a global pandemic. Even though the pandemic has inevitable impacts on the existing nationalist dynamics worldwide, it is still too early to posit whether it will ultimately promote or even impede the exclusionary tendency of nationalism (Bieber, 2020). This is because, under the current international order, we have been witnessing polarized social and institutional responses to confront the threat of an indiscriminative virus, which ranges from recessional measures that might make nationalism a more salient ideology and practice (that is, border closures and halted human migrations) to accelerated international cooperation that might demote nationalism while promoting transnational solidarity (that is, vaccination developments and international aids). Hence, this case further opens the speculation towards the world order in the post-pandemic era where complex socio-economic, political, and cultural fractures and fault lines largely co-exist.

Notes

[1] Those commentary articles collected as the empirical data for the chapter were circulated on WeChat and various China-language websites.

[2] All quotations presented in this paragraph are translated by the authors from the original Chinese version of Fang Fang's diaries. The Chinese version of these diaries cannot be found online now because they were deleted by Chinese censorship. However, the authors traced them back by using their own networks with some Chinese netizens.

[3] Quoted from www.reddit.com/r/China_irl/comments/fvrxlw/就方方的日记一个武汉人吐槽几句/

[4] Quoted from www.weibo.com/ttarticle/p/show?id=23096344931976938129113

[5] Quoted from www.hongqi.tv/zatan/2020-04-19/18037.html

[6] Quoted from www.ideobook.com/2931/fang-fang-diary

[7] Quoted from www.kunlunce.com/ssjj/guojipinglun/2020-04-10/142377.html

[8] Quoted from www.kunlunce.com/ssjj/guojipinglun/2020-04-10/142377.html

[9] Quoted from https://china.huanqiu.com/article/3xktVL9JRkI

[10] Quoted from https://k.sina.cn/article_5305757517_13c3f6f4d02000vl9b.html

[11] Quoted from www.hinabian.com/theme/detail/8331655740595442592.html

References

BBC News (2020) 'Fang Fang: the Wuhan writer whose virus diary angered China'. BBC News, www.bbc.com/news/world-asia-china-52712358

Bieber, F. (2020) 'Global nationalism in times of the COVID-19 pandemic'. *Nationalities Papers*, 1–13, DOI: 10.1017/nps.2020.35

Chen, T.C. (2010) 'China's reaction to the color revolutions: adaptive authoritarianism in full swing'. *Asian Perspective*, 34(2): 5–51.

Wasserstrom, J.N. (2008) 'China's political colours: from monochrome to palette'. *Open Democracy*, www.opendemocracy.net/en/china-s-political-colours-from-monochrome-to-palette/

Woods, E.T., Schertzer, R., Greenfeld, L., Hughes, C. and Miller-Idriss, C. (2020) 'COVID-19, nationalism, and the politics of crisis: a scholarly exchange'. *Nations and Nationalism*, 1–19, https://doi.org/10.1111/nana.12644

Xia, M. (2020) 'Fang Fang's Wuhan diaries are a personal account of shared memory'. *The Conversation*, https://theconversation.com/fang-fangs-wuhan-diaries-are-a-personal-account-of-shared-memory-138007

Ying, J. (2012) *Cyber-Nationalism in China: Challenging Western Media Portrayals of Internet Censorship in China*. Adelaide: University of Adelaide Press.

TEN

The COVID-19 Lockdown and the Impact of Poor-Quality Housing on Occupants in the UK

Philip Brown, Rachel Armitage, Leanne Monchuk, Dillon Newton, and Brian Robson

Introduction

The COVID-19 pandemic has impacted and transformed the lives of many people across the globe. An accurate understanding of the nature of these changes will take a number of years to materialize. What is clear, however, is the way housing has been elevated by the pandemic, not only in the way housing has been utilized by governments mandating populations to remain in their homes, but also in the role our homes play in our lives. It is clear that experiences of lockdown, and associated measures, will have been acutely influenced by housing. In particular, there will be distinct differences in experiences of lockdown depending on the availability of safe, secure, and decent accommodation. It is evident that people most at risk of experiencing the worst impacts of the pandemic, and the steps taken to mitigate the spread of the virus, are those already living with some form of pre–existing vulnerability, inequality, or precarity; in particular those in receipt of benefits, living with long-term conditions, in precarious employment, or those living in insecure housing or with poor housing conditions. As such, it is clear the experiences of people affected by multiple vulnerabilities should be documented and exposed (Gurney, 2020; Holmes et al, 2020; see also Tunstall, Chapter Two; Warnock, Chapter Twelve; Perry et al, Chapter Thirteen).

This chapter presents key findings from new rapid empirical research undertaken within the UK. Drawing on interviews with residents and professionals, we present the concerns, impacts, and lived experiences of respondents dealing with poor-quality housing.

Housing quality in the UK and its impacts

The quality of housing in the UK is variable across tenures and localities. The nature of the poorest-quality housing in the UK has been well established in the literature with data on its prevalence routinely collected as part of annual housing surveys. We are able to ascertain the proportion of dwellings which meet the Decent Homes Standard as recognized by indicators that assess homes for safety, state of repair, access and quality of facilities, and thermal comfort (Department for Communities and Local Government (DCLG), 2006). Housing quality issues tend to reside in the private-rented sector (PRS) followed by owner-occupation. Although there are shortcomings in the social housing sector, as a whole social housing is of high quality with the vast majority meeting the Standard. While housing surveys tend to show good levels of resident satisfaction with housing in general, there are a significant number of households who routinely deal with substandard conditions. For example, the latest English Housing Survey Headline Report revealed that in 2018, 12 percent of dwellings in the social rented sector failed to meet the Standard compared with 25 percent of PRS housing and 17 percent of owner-occupied homes (Ministry of Housing, Communities and Local Government (MHCLG),

2019). In the PRS, 14 percent of homes had a Category 1 hazard under the Housing Health and Safety Rating System (HHSRS); 11 percent of owner-occupied stock and 5 percent for social housing. Moreover, only 33 percent of PRS dwellings and 29 percent of owner-occupied dwellings have adequate levels of energy efficiency (Stephens et al, 2020).

While poor-quality housing is a national problem, the situation is acute in the North of England due to concentrations of pre-war, low-value properties. Recent work from The Smith Institute (2018) estimates that around 1 million owner-occupied homes in the North now fail to meet the Decent Homes Standard in addition to 354,000 private-rented homes. In turn, almost half of non-decent properties in the North contain someone over 60 or with a long-term health condition or disability. The impacts of poor housing conditions on health are well established (see Marmot Review, 2010) and it has been estimated that the annual cost to the NHS of poor housing is £1.4 billion (Buck and Gregory, 2018); a possible underestimation taking on board the impacts overcrowding and poor conditions have had on exposure to COVID-19 (Public Health England (PHE), 2020).

While the outcomes of housing inequalities have worsened because of COVID-19, the 'Stay at Home' message and subsequent adaptation measures prompted a reconfiguring of housing and 'home' for many. While some had little option but to spend more time exposed to hazardous conditions, others have spent time adapting to new working conditions in housing spaces. As debates are ongoing about the future role of traditional offices, the pandemic appears to have positioned housing and 'home' at the center of debates about the future of work and the role domestic space might play (see Hubbard, Chapter Four; Shearmur et al, Volume 4).

The research study

The research presented in this chapter was rapidly mobilized in late May 2020, and fieldwork was completed in late July

2020. The Project Team spoke to 50 households living in poor-quality housing and eight professionals who were working to support households throughout the pandemic. All interviews were undertaken via telephone, transcribed, and then analyzed using thematic coding and retrieval techniques with QSR NVivo software. We focused on people living in the private-rented and owner-occupied sectors. While we make no claim this sample is representative, we feel the stories collected are reflective of the broader experience of households living in the private-rented and owner-occupied sectors. The full report which expands on this methodology and provides comprehensive findings can be found at Brown et al (2020).

Research findings

Living with and repairing poor-quality housing

The residents we interviewed tended to be living with long-standing repair and quality issues. These ranged in severity and impact, with some having to manage relatively minor cosmetic faults that had become more apparent during lockdown, to major cases of damp, mold, and leaks which stemmed from significant structural issues. Lockdown had ultimately worsened such conditions due to a number of reasons. Many discussed how essential repair work to existing issues, due to be carried out by contractors, had been postponed; indeed, it was rare to hear accounts of people having contractors in homes to perform repairs. Others suggested that overuse of certain facilities had triggered sudden and unanticipated breakdowns of appliances, while some attributed inclement weather to leaks and observable damp and mold.

It was only in extreme cases such as the breakdown of heating systems when residents allowed contractors into properties. Sometimes the absence of contractors was a result of a disinclination to have outsiders in their living space for fear of infection. Others spoke about landlords reporting difficulties arranging for a contractor to visit. Some respondents suspected landlords were using lockdown as an excuse to postpone or delay costly repair works, whereas some landlords flatly refused to arrange repairs. Professionals had noticed a reduction in the number of complaints from households, although it was unclear, from their perspective, what was driving this. Organizations that provide specialized support to older adults living in owner-occupied accommodation were particularly concerned about the under-reporting of repairs and the impact this was having on already poor living standards and unsafe environments. This was a key concern looking towards the wetter and colder months of autumn and winter. Such factors led to the general view among professionals that once 'normality' had resumed there would be a significant backlog of issues and an unfavorable wider context in which these could be tackled.

Thermal comfort

Multiple residents discussed issues around thermal comfort, and this was a major theme in the research. Thermal comfort was discussed in terms of both the overheating of properties in particularly hot summer weeks exacerbated by having limited or no access to private outdoor space, and cold and damp conditions due to the inability of heating systems to retain heat for long durations of time. This was a significant feature in the interviews with low-income households, as well as with those people for whom the pandemic had added a new layer of uncertainty to their income and employment. It was clear that the inability to control thermal comfort, as well as energy costs, in the home was a particular source of anxiety.

Tenant–landlord relations

The UK private rented sector is largely unregulated. Over recent years there has been a growing focus on improving the management and compliance to standards of the sector as a result of pressure from major national housing and homelessness charities, tenants' unions and policy makers. Poor management characterizes the 'bottom end' of the private rented sector, and the pandemic has again exacerbated this. Whereas some renters commended the proactive approach their landlords had taken at the beginning of lockdown (to reassure tenants about their renting situation in light of impending job losses), others, which include those who had been made redundant or now had wages capped at 80 percent under the government's furlough scheme, perceived their landlords as lacking sympathy and compassion about their situation. The vast majority of renters had not pondered the possibility of asking landlords for rent reductions when questioned during interviews. Many were withholding the reality of their day-to-day experience in the home, not raising or chasing requests for fear of possible revenge evictions or deliberate rent increases.

Overcrowding and isolation

Nearly all residents talked about problems with overcrowding now that entire households were living, working, and spending time in the same housing space. Conversely, people who lived by themselves discussed feeling isolated and lonely in the weeks when contact with family and friends was restricted to online video call facilities. Loneliness and isolation were particularly acute for older adults and participants with health conditions who were at high-risk and could not, in any case, leave their dwellings, in line with the UK government's strategy to 'shield' the most vulnerable.

The psychological impact of living in poor-quality housing during the pandemic

The experience of containment over many weeks in poor-quality housing had a grinding effect on participants. For residents living in damp and moldy conditions, the development of chesty coughs took on a new dimension against a canvas of COVID-19. By virtue of being contained inside, others had come to face the bleak realities of their housing situations and the quality of properties they could afford. Whereas previously housing was a space in which very little time was spent due to work routines and unrestricted social lives, containment in low-quality housing had been forlorn experience for some households. The visibility of cracks in walls, the smell of damp, and the noise of dripping water from leaks being caught in buckets were discussed as now daily lived experiences. Households routinely reported the onset or resurgence of mental ill-health such as depression and anxiety. Households recounted coping strategies relating to both housing conditions and lockdown more generally which included practical strategies to psychological strategies. While a small proportion of households we spoke to were getting by, the findings suggest that the majority of households appeared to be living with a sense of dread about their future and their [in]ability to change it. There were heightened concerns about the precarity of their tenure, the frailty of their homes, the uncertainty of their financial situation, and a sense of impending hopelessness.

Conclusion

The findings from this study concur with the insight of others who have already commented on the COVID-19 pandemic as further exposing those living with existing vulnerabilities (Tunstall, Chapter Two; Warnock, Chapter Twelve; Xavier, Chapter Seven; Stevens, Chapter Eight; Banerjee and Das, Chapter Fifteen; Turman et al, Chapter Sixteen). The housing system in the UK has long been considered in a state of crisis (Bimpson and Goulding, 2020; Hubbard, Chapter Four). The drivers of this crisis are commonly seen as a mismatch between supply and demand and the increasing financialization of the housing sector. The number of privately rented homes in the UK has almost doubled in the last decade and now accommodates around 4.5 million households (Office for National Statistics (ONS), 2019). As rising house prices mean fewer people are able to purchase a home, and with social housing stock largely stagnant, private renting is no longer a short-term housing solution. This chapter has added to literature which wants to assert that the quality of existing housing is also a part of the current housing crisis. In addition, this chapter directly contributes to an understanding of the interconnected role housing plays within the context of public health and the health system more broadly.

The negative impacts of poor housing are evident and well established, the COVID-19 pandemic has made these impacts acute at a time of broader structural fragility. People living in poor housing conditions are more likely to experience increased mortality rates during the winter months as a result of respiratory, circulatory, and cardiovascular diseases, and are more likely to experience mental health conditions such as depression and anxiety. Evidence from this study suggests this is even more likely against the canvas of the pandemic. The housing stock in the North of England, even with the addition of newer dwellings over the last decade, remains characterized by older, colder, and poorly maintained properties. Housing quality issues did not begin with lockdown. Rather, households went into lockdown living in homes that were already in a poor state of repair. This accumulation of poor-quality housing represents a long-term failure of housing policy. Its presence implies the need for a long-term rebalancing of housing policy – at national, city-region, and local levels – so that the quality of our existing homes is treated as a priority equal to the importance of the supply of new homes.

Note

The authors wish to express gratitude to all those people who found time to speak with us during the course of the research, often under very challenging circumstances. We would also like to express our sincere gratitude to the funders for the research namely: the University of Huddersfield; The Northern Housing Consortium; and the Nationwide Foundation.

References

Bimpson, E. and Goulding, R. (2020) 'Housing crisis, austerity and the production of precarious lives', in J. Dobson and R. Atkinson (eds) *Urban Crisis, Urban Hope: A Policy Agenda for UK Cities*. London: Anthem, pp 23–8.

Brown, P., Newton, D., Armitage, R. and Monchuk, L. (2020) 'Lockdown. Rundown. Breakdown. The COVID-19 lockdown and the impact of poor-quality housing on occupants in the North of England'. Sunderland: Northern Housing Consortium.

Buck, D. and Gregory, S. (2018) *Housing and health opportunities for sustainability and transformation partnerships*. The Kings Fund, www.kingsfund.org.uk/sites/default/files/2018-03/Housing_and_health_final.pdf

Department for Communities and Local Government (DCLG) (2006) *A decent home: definition and guidance for implementation. June 2006 – update*. https://assets.publishing.service.gov.uk/government/uploads/system/uploads/attachment_data/file/7812/138355.pdf

Gurney, C. (2020) *Out of harm's way? Critical remarks on harm and the meaning of home during the 2020 COVID-19 social distancing measures*. Working paper, UK Collaborative Centre for Housing Evidence. https://housingevidence.ac.uk/wp-content/uploads/2020/04/200408-out-of-harms-way-craig-gurney-final.pdf

Holmes, E.A., O'Connor, R.C., Perry, V.H. et al (2020) 'Multidisciplinary research priorities for the COVID-19 pandemic: a call for action for mental health science'. *Lancet Psychiatry*, 7: 547–60, www.thelancet.com/pdfs/journals/lanpsy/PIIS2215-0366(20)30168-1.pdf

Marmot Review (2010) *Fair society, healthy lives: the Marmot Review: strategic review of health inequalities in England post-2010*. London: Institute of Health Equity.

Ministry of Housing, Communities and Local Government (MHCLG) (2019) *English housing survey: headline report, 2018–19*. HMSO, https://assets.publishing.service.gov.uk/government/uploads/system/uploads/attachment_data/file/860076/2018-19_EHS_Headline_Report.pdf

Office for National Statistics (ONS) (2019) *UK private-rented sector: 2018*, www.ons.gov.uk/economy/inflationandpriceindices/articles/ukprivaterentedsector/2018#things-you-need-to-know

Public Health England (PHE) (2020) *Beyond the data: understanding the impact of COVID-19 on BAME groups*, https://assets.publishing.service.gov.uk/government/uploads/system/uploads/attachment_data/file/892376/COVID_stakeholder_engagement_synthesis_beyond_the_data.pdf

Stephens, M., Perry, J., Williams, P., Young, G. and Fitzpatrick, S. (eds) (2020) *UK Housing Review 2020* [28th edn]. Coventry: Chartered Institute of Housing.

The Smith Institute (2018) *The hidden costs of poor-quality housing in the North*. Northern Housing Consortium, www.northern-consortium.org.uk/wp-content/uploads/2018/10/The-Hidden-Costs-of-Poor-Quality-Housing-in-the-North.pdf

ELEVEN

Aging at Home: The Elderly in Gauteng, South Africa in the Context of COVID-19

Alexandra Parker and Julia de Kadt

Introduction

The Gauteng city-region (GCR), South Africa's economic hub and home to over 15 million people, is currently facing two epidemics. One is COVID-19, and the other is HIV/AIDS. With just under 2 million people living with HIV/ AIDS in the GCR (Simbayi et al, 2019) and the largest HIV-positive population of any city in the world (Stuart et al, 2018), HIV/ AIDS has substantially impacted the demographics of the GCR, and the structure of families and households. Through these shifts, HIV/AIDS has placed a disproportionate burden of caregiving and financial support on the elderly. Our analysis explores the ways in which the arrival of COVID-19 interacts with Gauteng's demographic and social fabric to further deepen the burdens of care and support experienced by the province's elderly (see also Lemanski and De Groot, Volume 1).

Overall, 9.1 percent of South Africa's population is over 60 years of age, which is higher than most other African countries (Ausubel, 2020). The GCR has a slightly lower proportion of those over 60, at 8.46 percent (StatsSA, 2020). One of the main reasons for this is the legacy of South Africa's history of apartheid-driven labor migration (Moore and Seekings, 2018). Apartheid legislation restricted Black African residence in urban areas largely to those of working age, resulting in profound divisions of families across rural and urban areas. Although the legislation was repealed in the late 1980s, many older people continue to leave the GCR on retirement. South Africa's higher proportion of elderly relates to the relative affluence of the country in the African context, but also to the HIV/AIDS epidemic, which, particularly prior to the introduction of treatment in 2004, resulted in the premature death of many younger people (Udjo, 2006).

South Africa's demography and history of circular migration leaves many elderly family members caring for their grandchildren in 'skip generation' households (where parents are missing). Extended living arrangements and co-residence with adult children is common, and since the 1990s has been further encouraged through the implementation of a universal old-age grant paid to all those over 60 without an alternative income source. These grants make elderly residents attractive to households, and, while broadly beneficial, can result in the dependence of younger family members, or contribute to intergenerational conflict (Moore and Seekings, 2018).

While deterioration in health is expected with aging, South Africa's elderly have, overall, particularly poor health. The prevalence of HIV in adults aged 50 years and older is high: it is 12.5 percent nationally, and slightly lower at 11.1 percent in Gauteng (Simbayi et al, 2019). Hypertension and diabetes are widespread, particularly in urban areas, and the mortality rate from seasonal influenza is substantially higher for South

Africa's elderly in comparison to the United States (Cohen et al, 2010). Additionally, Gauteng's many mine dumps have caused higher prevalence of 'chronic respiratory symptoms and diseases among the elderly in communities located near mine dumps' (Nkosi et al, 2015: 7).

The susceptibility of the elderly to COVID-19, and their broader vulnerability in the context of the pandemic, may be exacerbated by poor mental health. Mental health problems, which in South Africa, as elsewhere, are more prevalent among the elderly than the general population (Hao et al, 2017), can exacerbate the symptoms of some diseases, and can cause premature death (Plagg et al, 2020). Internationally, several studies show that the mental health of the elderly has deteriorated during the pandemic with higher levels of depression and anxiety (Meng et al, 2020) and an increase in suicide rates (Monteiro-Junior et al, 2020). These figures are likely not unrelated to the outbreak of ageism in response to the pandemic, with the contribution of the elderly to society being brought into question (Ayalon et al, 2020).

Globally, the increased vulnerability of the elderly to severe symptoms or death from COVID-19 is well documented. In South Africa, this biological vulnerability interacts with demographic structure, and the particular social and economic burdens borne by the elderly, to shape the risks faced by this group. This is exacerbated by extensive economic hardship and social distress in the wake of COVID-19. We use data from the Gauteng City-Region Observatory's (GCRO) Quality of Life Survey V 2017–18) (QoL V) (GCRO, 2019) to better understand the lives of the elderly in the GCR. In particular, we look at how the elderly form part of families and households, and fulfill key caregiving and economic roles in the province. Understanding these roles, heavily shaped by the HIV/AIDS epidemic, is critical to understanding – and working to mitigate – the particular implications of the COVID-19 pandemic on the GCR's elderly, and the GCR itself.

Methods and analysis

For this chapter, we draw on the QoL V data (GCRO, 2019), which consists of 24,889 interviews with randomly sampled adult respondents at their homes, across all areas of the GCR. The data is weighted to the gender and population group distribution of adult GCR residents. We have defined the elderly as those aged 60 and above, in recognition of South Africa's relatively low average life expectancy, high levels of both communicable and non-communicable illness, and a relatively weak health system. Overall, some 13 percent of survey respondents in Gauteng are aged 60 years and older (n=3350), suggestive of slight oversampling.

Due to South Africa's apartheid legacy, White[1] residents continue to have much better living conditions than Black Africans. Whites also have a substantially longer life expectancy, meaning that they constitute a higher proportion of the elderly than of the population as a whole (StatsSA, 2020). As Black Africans make up the large majority (79 percent) of Gauteng's population, and on average experience the most challenging living conditions, we have focused our analysis exclusively on the elderly in this population group (n=2245).

To better understand the vulnerabilities faced by older Black Africans in Gauteng with regard to COVID-19, we examined a range of variables covering living conditions, health vulnerabilities, and roles within families and households. Our analysis was informed by the syndemics approach, which emphasizes the relationship between disease progression and social and environmental factors (Singer et al, 2017). Variables selected focus on the extent to which living conditions and infrastructure support appropriate social distance and preventative hygiene: measuring absence of piped water; shared or inadequate toilet facilities; and living in a crowded dwelling. Variables measuring health vulnerability include pre-existing health conditions in the household, poor health status, mental health, and dependence on public health care services.

We found that overall, the older Black African's living conditions are better suited to maintaining social distancing and preventative hygiene, in comparison to younger adults. They are less likely to live in crowded conditions (10 percent compared with 18 percent for younger adults)[2] and less likely to have shared sanitation (16 percent compared to 9 percent), or shared access to water (11 percent compared to 5 percent). However, their increased health risks are clear: they are more likely to live in households with pre-existing health conditions that exacerbate the symptoms of COVID-19 (66 percent compared to 27 percent) and are more likely to report poor health status (23 percent compared to 5 percent). They are also more likely to rely on public health care services (87 percent compared to 76 percent). The GCR's elderly also struggle more with depression than the working-age adult population – 17 percent of the elderly have PHQ-2 scores indicative of a high probability of clinical depression, compared to 12 percent of younger adults.

While their slightly better living conditions may offer the elderly some protection from COVID-19 infection, their physical and mental health are likely to substantially increase their broader vulnerability. These vulnerabilities have likely been exacerbated by interruptions in health care services for chronic care, and potentially, social isolation resulting from South Africa's lengthy and strict lockdown.

However, only 21 percent of elderly Black Africans live alone, with most (79 percent) living in households with two or more people. Of those living in a two-person household, only 40 percent live with their spouse. Of the elderly not living alone, most live with family members other than their spouse (60 percent), and more than half (54 percent) live in households including children under 18 years.

Not only do the elderly often live with children, but they frequently support children financially, including their own adult children. Nearly three quarters (74 percent) of Black African elderly respondents reported having at least one dependent child, and those with dependent children had an average of 3.3. These children include both minors and adults, and support roles may include daily caregiving, provision of food and shelter, or simply financial support.

Of elderly Black African respondents who report having dependent children, 88 percent fulfill the role of primary carer – that makes up 65 percent of all elders. Furthermore, 27 percent of these older respondents live with their own children who are younger than 18 years, while 40 percent live with their adult children. In addition, many (32 percent) live with their grandchildren, with 49 percent of this group in 'skip generation' households and 51 percent in multi-generation households. Clearly, many of Gauteng's elderly are playing a significant role with regard to the care and support of children, both minor and adult.

Elder-headed households are likely to be particularly vulnerable in the context of the COVID-19 pandemic, particularly through illness or death of the household head. Some 13.5 percent of household heads in the GCR are elderly. Of elderly Black African respondents, 87 percent identify themselves as the head of their household – suggesting that they are probably making financial contributions, likely through their pension or old-age grant.

Conclusion

While the GCR has a slightly lower proportion of elderly residents than other regions of South Africa, their vulnerability in the context of COVID-19 remains a crucial consideration. We demonstrate that the elderly are particularly vulnerable in terms of both physical and mental health, but that compared to younger respondents they may be better situated to absorb some of the socio-economic shocks of the pandemic (see also Hartt et al, Volume 4; Lindenberg et al, Volume 2). Given high HIV prevalence levels, many of the elderly are themselves HIV positive, or caring for affected relatives. In a context of high unemployment and low wages, the elderly also play a key role in supporting childcare for wage earners in the GCR, and their grant income provides a crucial financial input into many households. These factors shape the elderly's risk of exposure to COVID-19, but also highlight the risks faced by families, and society more broadly, when the elderly become infected with COVID-19.

The COVID-19 pandemic has the potential to significantly impact many households that include, or rely on support from, elderly household members. Household structure must be considered as part of any preventative measure. While removing the elderly from multi-generational households would likely be inordinately harmful, guidance can be provided on how to appropriately manage risks, and support effective isolation or quarantine when necessary. Financial and social support mechanisms for households who lose an elderly member are also critical, and must be responsive to the diversity of living situations and household structures across the region.

The lives of Gauteng's elderly are almost certainly intertwined with those of younger residents in numerous other ways beyond those presented here. Along with the pandemic's economic and social costs, the human and emotional impacts of allowing COVID-19 to disrupt large numbers of intergenerational relationships in a short period of time will be substantial, and devastating. The importance of protecting and supporting Gauteng's elderly and their dependents is clear.

Notes

[1] We use the population group descriptors used in the official South African census, capitalised to reflect recent shifts in terminology usage.

[2] The differences in figures presented in this section are all significant at $p < 0.001$.

References

Ausubel, J. (2020) 'Populations skew older in some of the countries hit hard by COVID-19', Pew Research Center, April 22, https://pewrsr.ch/2KqdZwF

Ayalon, L., Chasteen, A., Diehl, M., Levy, B.R., Neupert, S.D., Rothermund, K., Tesch-Römer, C. and Wahl, H.-W. (2020) 'Aging in times of the COVID-19 pandemic: avoiding ageism and fostering intergenerational solidarity'. *The Journals of Gerontology: Series B*, 76(2): e49–52, https://doi.org/10.1093/geronb/gbaa051

Cohen, C., Simonsen, L., Kang, J., Miller, M., McAnerney, J., Blumberg, L., Schoub, B., Madhi, S.A. and Viboud, C. (2010) 'Elevated influenza-related excess mortality in South African elderly individuals, 1998–2005'. *Clinical Infectious Diseases*, 51(12): 1362–9, https://doi.org/10.1086/657314

Gauteng City-Region Observatory (GCRO) (2019) Quality of life survey V 2017–18 [Dataset]. Version 1. Johannesburg and Cape Town: GCRO & DataFirst, https://doi.org/10.25828/8yf7-9261

Hao, G., Bishwajit, G., Tang, S., Nie, C., Ji, L. and Huang, R. (2017) 'Social participation and perceived depression among elderly population in South Africa'. *Clinical Interventions in Aging*, 12: 971–6, https://doi.org/10.2147/CIA.S137993

Meng, H., Xu, Y., Dai, J., Zhang, Y., Liu, B. and Yang, H. (2020) 'Analyze the psychological impact of COVID-19 among the elderly population in China and make corresponding suggestions'. *Psychiatry Research*, 289: 112983, https://doi.org/10.1016/j.psychres.2020.112983

Monteiro-Junior, R.S., Carneiro, L.S.F., Barca, M.L., Kristiansen, K.M., Sampaio, C.A., Haikal, D.S., Antunes, L., Leão, L.L. and Deslandes, A.C. (2020) 'COVID-19 pandemic: a multinational report providing professional experiences in the management of mental health of elderly'. *International Psychogeriatrics*, 1–4, https://doi.org/10.1017/S1041610220001027

Moore, E. and Seekings, J. (2018) 'Social protection, intergenerational relationships and conflict in South Africa'. Centre for Social Science Research, CSSR Working Paper No. 419.

Nkosi, V., Wichmann, J. and Voyi, K. (2015) 'Chronic respiratory disease among the elderly in South Africa: any association with proximity to mine dumps?' *Environmental Health*, 14(1): 33, https://doi.org/10.1186/s12940-015-0018-7

Plagg, B., Engl, A., Piccoliori, G. and Eisendle, K. (2020) 'Prolonged social isolation of the elderly during COVID-19: between benefit and damage'. *Archives of Gerontology and Geriatrics*, 89: 104086, https://doi.org/10.1016/j.archger.2020.104086

Simbayi, L., Zuma, K., Zungu, N., Moyo, S., Marinda, E., Jooste, S., Mabaso, M., Ramlagan, S., North, A., Van Zyl, J. and Mohlabane, N. (2019) *South African National HIV Prevalence, Incidence, Behaviour and Communication Survey, 2017: Towards Achieving the UNAIDS 90-90-90 Targets*. Cape Town: HSRC Press.

Singer, M., Bulled, N., Ostrach, B. and Mendenhall, E. (2017) 'Syndemics and the biosocial conception of health'. *The Lancet*, 389(10072): 941–50.

StatsSA (2020) *Mid-year population estimates 2020*. Statistics South Africa, Statistical Release, P0302.

Stuart, R., Fraser-Hurt, N., Kerr, C. et al (2018) 'The city of Johannesburg can end AIDS by 2030: modelling the impact of achieving the fast-track targets and what it will take to get there'. *Journal of the International Aids Society*, 21: e25068.

Udjo, E.O. (2006) 'Demographic impact of HIV/AIDS on the young and elderly populations in South Africa'. *Journal of Intergenerational Relationships*, 4(2): 23–41, https://doi.org/10.1300/J194v04n02_03

TWELVE

COVID-19, Lockdown(s), and Housing Inequalities among Families with Autistic Children in London

Rosalie Warnock

Introduction

Living through lockdown is particularly challenging for families who have children with autism.[1] People may be disabled by their autism in different ways and to varying degrees (some with co-occurring conditions), thus experiences of the COVID-19 pandemic will have varied between people and families. This is not because of autism per se, but due to social, spatial, and economic inequalities between families. During lockdown, the home has been the primary location where these differences are lived and felt.

Drawing on research with London-based parents who have autistic children,[2] this chapter highlights pre-existing housing inequalities which have exacerbated the challenges for many of managing the COVID-19 lockdowns (see also Tunstall, Chapter Two; Kayanan et al, Chapter Seventeen; Graham et al, Volume 1). The chapter raises issues of space, safety, and care in and out of the home. Learning from COVID-19 and in antici-pation of future pandemics, it makes two recommendations. First, the appropriate allocation of social housing where neces-sary to families who have disabled children. Second, adequate financial and practical support for adult and young carers, who continue to bear the brunt of inadequate social care in the UK.

Disability, housing needs, and housing inequalities

Housing inequalities matter for children with autism and their families. Autism affects people across the socio-economic spectrum and from all ethnicities and nationalities, but some children and their families are more likely to be living in unsuitable housing than others. Housing data on families with disabled children are scant (Provan et al, 2016), however, figures suggest that while 19 percent of UK families live in poverty, 26 percent of households with a disabled child and 40 percent of households with a disabled adult *and* a disabled child live in poverty (Joseph Rowntree Foundation (JRF), 2020: 57).

Living with a disability is expensive (JRF, 2020) and impacts on some disabled adults and carers' abilities to work. Income has implications for housing options (social or pri-vate rented, homeownership) and housing size (larger prop-erties and/or outdoor space tends to be more expensive). Since Right to Buy legislation (Housing Act, 1980)[3] social housing availability has plummeted, pushing many into the private-rental sector (Shelter, nd). In England, 54 percent of socially renting households have at least one member who is disabled or has a long-term illness, compared with 23 percent of privately renting households and 31 percent of owner-occupier households (2017–18 figures, Ministry of Housing, Communities & Local Government (MHCLG), 2019: 3). While 8 percent of social renters and 6 percent of private renters in England live in overcrowded accommodation (Wilson and Barton, 2020: 6), families across Britain with a disabled child are

50 percent more likely to experience overcrowding than those with non-disabled children (Beresford and Rhodes, 2008).

A shortage of accessible social housing in the UK across all tenures keeps families with disabled children in unsuitable housing for longer. Disabled children and young people are more likely to spend more time at home than those without disabilities, but their homes are often 'the most restrictive environments in which they spend their time' (Beresford and Rhodes, 2008). During the COVID-19 lockdowns, disabled children have been forced to spend even more time than usual in restrictive home spaces. For those with autism, this could also include not having enough physical space to play or sleep alone, not being able to play independently due to safety concerns, or sensory issues with their home environment. Some may also struggle with inaccessible entrances, stairs, and bathroom facilities.

Rates of social renting vary by ethnicity in the UK (Gov.uk, 2020) – a sign of systemic racial and structural inequality – with racially minoritized[4] households more likely to experience overcrowding than White British households (Wilson and Barton, 2020). As flats outnumber houses in social renting stock, so the higher proportion of Black and Asian families living in socially rented housing are more likely to live in medium- and high-rise flats (Gulliver, 2017). Black, Asian, and racially minoritized children are four times less likely to have access to outdoor space than White children (Gilhooly, 2020). This matters when examining variations in autistic children and their families' experiences of indoor and outdoor space during the COVID-19 lockdown.

In London, only 66 percent of children have access to a private garden, while 5 percent do not have any access to outdoor space (private garden, balcony, or communal garden) at all (Gilhooly, 2020). While 44 percent of Londoners live within a five-minute walk from a park (Office for National Statistics (ONS), 2020) over half of Londoners still do not have easy access to good-quality green space. Parents of children with autism may be additionally restricted by safety concerns when traveling to and using public green space.

The COVID-19 lockdowns for families of children with autism

While families face different challenges during lockdown, enforced and extended indoor confinement makes housing critical. The pandemic has demonstrated that unsuitable home environments make caring harder.

Space

The first issue for most families is space. In this research, even homeowning families spoke of a lack of space, but overcrowding was most severe among social renting families. 'Lucy', who identified as 'Black and White EU', lived in a one-bed flat with her eight-year-old son. They had been on the waiting list for a bigger flat since he was born. 'Donna', who identified as British Bangladeshi, lived in a three-bed flat with her three children (aged 20, 19, and 6). She shared a bedroom with her youngest daughter, who had autism, and was waiting for a bigger property. 'Brianna', who identified as Black British, lived with her partner and three autistic children (aged 21, six, and three) in a two-bed flat. Her, her partner, and two youngest children shared one bedroom. After a six-year wait, Brianna was offered a four-bedroom house with a garden as our interviews finished. But at the time of research, all three mothers shared bedrooms with children who had difficulties sleeping (common for people with autism). This impacted on their own abilities to sleep and to function day-to-day. Sleep deprivation affects parents and carers' mental and physical energy, making childcare, paid employment, and managing children's appointments and paperwork additionally challenging.

Overcrowded housing prevents parents and carers from establishing suitable routines for their autistic children. For example, if children share bedrooms or do not have their own safe space to retreat to, it can impact on their mental health and increase their risk of becoming dysregulated, meaning they, their parents or carers, and siblings, struggle further. While lockdown has been unsettling for most children, those with autism may have struggled even more so to understand what is going on. In a survey by the Disabled Children's Partnership (DCP), 78 percent of respondents said the COVID-19 lockdown had negatively impacted their disabled child's mental health (2020: 7). The risk of children having meltdowns has been exacerbated by the pandemic, which has disrupted normal routines and confined families to the home. For some autistic children, re-learning rules about what is 'safe' and 'unsafe' may have resulted in them becoming too anxious of the outside world to leave their home at all.

Safety

The second issue – highlighted by these meltdowns – is safety. While there are separate housing assessment processes for households with a disabled member, social housing shortages mean that families are often placed in unsuitable housing. This ranges from flats in medium- and high-rise buildings with open balconies, to temporary accommodation in shared houses or B&Bs. While Lucy had an occupational therapy report stating that they needed a ground-floor flat, she lived in a second-floor flat and had installed an alarm system on her front door to alert her if her son tried to leave the house. Donna lived in a third-floor flat where she could not open any windows when her youngest daughter was home, meaning Donna could only cook when she was out. Brianna explained that she could not even go to the toilet without expecting to come back to find 'trauma'. Her middle son had pica in addition to autism; a condition causing him to chew non-food items. This meant she could not leave him unattended in case he chewed wires or choked on something.

In multi-generational households, pre-existing challenges with regard to space and generational differences in need (see Taylor, 2021) are likely to have been complicated by the need to shield older or immunocompromised family members, while also caring for disabled children. For families living in overcrowded and/or unsafe houses without gardens, these decisions become even harder as parents and carers are forced to weigh up the least bad option, between remaining indoors or risking infection outside.

Spending time outside can help families to manage unsuitable housing. Crucially, neither Donna nor Brianna (at the time) had access to either a private or shared garden, and Lucy only had access to public green space outside her block of flats. In a city like London where domestic life unfolds between home and city spaces, for example in parks and public squares (Koch and Latham, 2012; Blunt and Sheringham, 2019; see also Dobson, Volume 3; Whitten and Massini, Volume 3; Rodrigues et al, Volume 3), lockdown restrictions pose new challenges. Donna spoke of periods where she had taken her daughter to the park four times a day to blow off energy. Lucy and her son went on frequent walks and bike rides because it was free, emphasizing how low-income families rely on outside spaces that do not cost money.

However, not all families can access free outdoor space easily or safely. Donna and Lucy lived within reasonable distance of nearby parks and each only had one child to take and look after. However, for parents like Brianna, whose daughter refused to walk outside the house and used a buggy (common among children with autism) and whose son was also reluctant to walk outside, going to the park can become much harder.

Early lockdown restrictions limiting people to one daily trip outside and nearby caused problems for parents and carers who take their children (sometimes by car) to safe, remote, outdoor places, often multiple times per day (Walker, 2020). For autistic children who run off, or with sensory needs who scream or shout, this can be a crucial coping mechanism to ensure their child's physical and mental well-being, while minimizing stressful noise complaints from unsupportive neighbors. Following legal action, these restrictions were eased early on for people with autism and learning disabilities (Walker, 2020). However, if children cannot abide by social distancing rules, or might touch, lick, or bite things for sensory reasons (as Brianna's son did), some parents may still decide it is unsafe to leave the house. Lucy, Donna, and Brianna did not own cars. Families who cannot safely walk to a park – particularly those whose children use buggies – may be unable to reach outdoor space without taking public transport, and may decide is not worth the risk.

Care

This brings us to the third issue: care. As a result of either school closures or decisions not to send children to school (due to shielding or safety concerns), many parents and carers have found themselves supervising disabled children 24/7, without the normal respite that school hours or their own work usually brings. While this has been challenging for all parents and carers, it has been particularly difficult for those caring for children with additional needs. Most UK schools have remained open for vulnerable children and key workers' children, but not all mainstream schools have been able to accommodate all pupils who have special educational needs and disabilities (SEND) and not all specialist schools have been able to operate safely at full capacity (Weale, 2020). Additionally, face-to-face therapy sessions have moved online, and respite care stopped for most (Hill, 2020; DCP, 2020).

For parents and carers who work, balancing home-schooling and full-time care for children has been challenging. While some have tried to work from home, those employed as key workers might not have been able to. Working parents left without their usual respite care (Hill, 2020) may have had to consider giving up their jobs and subsequently, their financial security. This dilemma has hit single parents especially. Donna worked 16 hours per week and used her 'short breaks' council money to pay for a respite carer for her younger daughter while she worked during school holidays. When this money ran out, she relied on her 18-year-old daughter to care for her sister. However, her eldest daughter was so scared of her sister having an accident under her watch that she refused to take her out of the house on her own.

While we do not know what decision Donna took during lockdown, we must consider the impact that the pandemic has had on siblings of children with autism who act as young carers. Parents and carers report being on the 'brink of collapse' without respite care (Hill, 2020) – leaving siblings to help fill the gaps. During the first COVID-19 lockdown, 58 percent of surveyed young carers (aged 12–15) and 64 percent of young adult carers (aged 16–25) reported that the amount of time they spent caring (for parents, siblings, or others) had increased since the pandemic started (Carers Trust, 2020: 5). With no school, restrictions on leaving the house, and for young carers who share bedrooms, there may be little-to-no respite from responsibilities at home, as COVID-19 continues indefinitely.

Policy recommendations: housing and social care

This research has demonstrated the difficulties of caring for an autistic child when confined to an unsuitable home. Two points should inform future housing and social policy. First, it is essential that social housing is allocated appropriately for families who have disabled children. Properties should be safe, with an appropriate number of bedrooms, and should be on the ground floor with accessible entrances and private, enclosed gardens wherever possible. This is of course part of a longer-term national imperative to build more housing for social and affordable rent – which must include a commitment to tackling intersecting inequalities in housing tenures. Where social or affordable rented housing is part of private developments, free access to on-site outdoor spaces must be guaranteed.

Second, the COVID-19 pandemic has highlighted the additional daily challenges of caring for a disabled child. It is imperative that adult and young carers are properly supported, by raising the rate of carers allowance to recognize caring as a full-time job, providing adequate respite care, and considering introducing a national care service in the UK.

Notes

[1] While recognising that there is debate within the autism community about using person-first versus identity-first language, both 'children with autism' and 'autistic children' are used in this chapter to recognise variation in participants' preferred descriptors for themselves and their children.

[2] Research was conducted in 2019, using in-depth narrative inquiry methods with 14 London-based families who had autistic children. Eight families lived in socially rented housing, one rented privately, and five were homeowners. Names have been changed.

[3] The Housing Act (1980) gave local authority and other social renting tenants the 'Right to Buy' their homes for the first time, while also restricting local authorities' ability to build replacement council-owned housing.

[4] With Gunaratnam (2003) and following Milner and Jumbe (2020: e419), I use the term 'racially minoritized' to recognize that people are actively minoritized by others, rather than naturally being a minority.

References

Beresford, B. and Rhodes, D. (2008) *Housing and disabled children*, Joseph Rowntree Foundation, June 6, www.jrf.org.uk/report/housing-and-disabled-children

Blunt, A. and Sheringham, O. (2019) 'Home-city geographies: urban dwelling and mobility'. *Progress in Human Geography*, 43(5): 815–34, https://doi.org/10.1177/0309132518786590

Carers Trust (2020) *My future, my feelings, my family: how Coronavirus is affecting young carers and young adult carers, and what they want you to do next*. https://carers.org/downloads/what-we-do-section/my-future-my-feelings-my-family.pdf

Disabled Children's Partnership (DCP) (2020) *#LeftInLockdown – Parent carers' experiences of lockdown*. https://disabledchildrenspartnership. org.uk/wp-content/uploads/2020/06/LeftInLockdown-Parent-carers%E2%80%99-experiences-of-lockdown-June-2020.pdf

Gilhooly, R. (2020) *How lockdown has affected children's lives at home*. Children's Commissioner, August 22, www.childrenscommissioner. gov.uk/2020/08/22/how-lockdown-has-affected-childrens-lives-at-home/

Gov.uk (2020) *Renting social housing*. UK Government, February 4, www.ethnicity-facts-figures.service.gov.uk/housing/social-housing/renting-from-a-local-authority-or-housing-association-social-housing/latest#by-ethnicity-and-area

Gulliver, K. (2017) *Forty years of struggle: a window on race and housing, disadvantage and exclusion*. Human City, https://humancityinstitute. files.wordpress.com/2017/01/forty-years-of-struggle.pdf

Gunaratnam, Y. (2003) *Researching Race and Ethnicity: Methods, Knowledge and Power*. London: Sage.

Hill, A. (2020) '"Brink of collapse": parents of disabled children buckling under 24-hour care'. *The Guardian*, May 13, www.theguardian.com/society/2020/may/13/parents-disabled-children-buckling-under-24-hour-care-coronavirus

Housing Act (1980) c.51. www.legislation.gov.uk/ukpga/1980/51

Joseph Rowntree Foundation (JRF) (2020) *UK Poverty 2019/20*, www.jrf.org.uk/report/uk-poverty-2019-20

Koch, R. and Latham, A. (2012) 'On the hard work of domesticating a public space'. *Urban Studies*, 50(1): 6–21, https://doi. org/10.1177/0042098012447001

Milner, A. and Jumbe, S. (2020) 'Using the right words to address racial disparities in COVID-19'. *The Lancet*, 5(8), https://doi. org/10.1016/S2468-2667(20)30162-6

Ministry of Housing, Communities & Local Government (MHCLG) (2019) *English housing survey: social rented sector, 2017–18*, https:// assets.publishing.service.gov.uk/government/uploads/system/ uploads/attachment_data/file/856046/EHS_2017-18_SRS_ report_revised.pdf

Office for National Statistics (ONS) (2020) *One in eight British households has no garden*, May 14, www.ons.gov.uk/economy/environmentalaccounts/articles/oneineightbritishhouseholdshasnogarden/2020-05-14

Provan, B., Burchardt, T. and Suh, E. (2016) *No place like an accessible home: quality of life and opportunity for disabled people with accessible housing needs.* CASE report 109. London: LSE, www.lse.ac.uk/business-and-consultancy/consulting/assets/documents/No-Place-Like-an-Accessible-Home.pdf

Shelter (nd) *Building for our future. A vision for social housing: the final report of Shelter's commission on the future of social housing*, https://england.shelter.org.uk/__data/assets/pdf_file/0005/1642613/Shelter_UK_-_A_vision_for_social_housing_full_interactive_report.pdf

Taylor, F.M. (2021) 'Cumulative precarity: millennial experience and multigenerational cohabitation in Hackney, London'. *Antipode*, 53(2): 587–606, https://doi.org/10.1111/anti.12689

Walker, A. (2020) 'UK coronavirus rules relaxed for people with autism and learning disabilities'. *The Guardian*, April 14, www.theguardian.com/world/2020/apr/14/uk-coronavirus-rules-autism-learning-disabilities-lockdown

Weale, S. (2020) 'English schools "using coronavirus as excuse" not to teach special needs pupils'. *The Guardian*, July 1, www.theguardian.com/education/2020/jul/01/english-schools-using-coronavirus-as-excuse-not-to-teach-special-needs-pupils

Wilson, W. and Barton, C. (2020) *Overcrowded housing (England).* Briefing paper number 1013. London: House of Commons Library, https://commonslibrary.parliament.uk/research-briefings/sn01013/

THIRTEEN

Detroit's Work to Address the Pandemic for Older Adults: A City of Challenge, History, and Resilience

Tam E. Perry, James McQuaid, Claudia Sanford, and Dennis Archambault

Introduction

When the coronavirus hit in March, it threw everybody for a loop. Some people were bedridden ... it was very hard on them. Everyone was locked in, like they were in prison. We couldn't visit each other, see each other. I talk on the phone, which is what I do most of the time. We had quite a few seniors pass. (Danielle Masters)[1]

Tenant organizers and other low-income senior housing advocates with the Senior Housing Preservation – Detroit (SHP-D) coalition were shocked to learn that several building managers took leave without establishing safety precautions for congregate housing. This coalition had a new purpose in the pandemic and convened to discuss issues that continued to go unaddressed. Founded in 2013 as a coalition of 15 organizations fighting for the preservation of subsidized, low-income senior housing in Detroit, SHP-D has a three-pronged mission: first, SHP-D works to preserve existing low-income housing for seniors in the face of displacement; second, SHP-D devotes time and resources for seniors who, despite their long terms of residency, are forced from their homes by development; and third, SHP-D seeks to preserve the intergenerational character of rapidly changing neighborhoods in Detroit (Perry et al, 2015; Perry et al, 2017). Coalition members worked together throughout 2020 to meet the coalition's strategic plan (see Perry et al, 2020 for more detail on the development of the strategic plan) of 1) understanding the changing context, 2) advocacy, and 3) making connections applied to a worldwide pandemic. This chapter written by three of the coalition's members and a doctoral student in history integrates their own perspectives and work in the City of Detroit. Tam Perry is a social work faculty member at Wayne State University in midtown Detroit and focused on the intersection of macro social work and gerontology; Claudia Sanford is a tenant organizer at the prominent housing agency, United Community Housing Coalition and offers on-the-ground perspectives in her multiple interactions in senior buildings; and Dennis Archambault of the Detroit Wayne County Health Authority champions the integration of health concerns in addressing the needs of those in senior buildings. James McQuaid's grounding in Detroit's history adds to the chapter as well.

This chapter is organized to highlight the voices of older Detroiters, describe the city's senior housing context, reflect on Detroit's history of housing struggle, and advocate for the continued need for housing solutions for all ages (for other examples of partnership, see Turman et al, Chapter Sixteen; for seniors' experiences during the pandemic, see Lindenberg et al, Volume 1; Nagesh et al, Volume 1; Low and Loukaitou-Sideris, Volume 3; Osborne et al, Volume 3; Hartt et al, Volume 4).

All of the people here are scared. Everyone stays to themselves. They're locked up in their apartments. They only come out when they have to come out. We don't socialize like we used to socialize … They have fear for their health. Some of them, like myself, have pre-existing conditions. We're in the high-risk category. (Clyde Lane)

Seniors often procured essentials by taking public transportation, which compounded risks for this already vulnerable age group, and weeks later, there was still no dedicated food or essential grocery distribution system for these seniors. Through key actions of Claudia Sanford, tenant organizer with the United Community Housing Coalition (UCHC) and chair of SHP-D, PPE, food and hygiene boxes, and needed public health information were finally delivered to select apartment buildings. The Michigan Center for Urban African American Aging Research conducted wellness calls to identify seniors with immediate needs and reduce social isolation, which has a known impact on health and well-being. Of the 557 surveys conducted, nearly half rated their current experience as at least somewhat stressful. Only 165 claimed to have three or four friends they could hear from or see at least once a month (Rorai and Perry, 2020).

As the scope of the pandemic on the Detroit community has become known (by September 14, 2020, an estimated 1,630 Detroiters had lost their lives), seniors in the city have demonstrated unyielding resilience (Detroit Health Department, 2020). Older residents saw friends and family hospitalized and die. As Detroit suffered greatly at the start of the pandemic, seniors developed ways to cope with health challenges in a city where many have had to contend with disparities in health care, sporadic employment histories, and racist hiring and lending practices. They are now telling the story of a forgotten population in the COVID-19 pandemic.

Intersection of age and spatial inequity: preserving senior housing in a changing city

Amid Detroit's 2013 bankruptcy and subsequent restructuring, many of the city's social services and regulations were eliminated through the actions of a state-appointed emergency manager. Detroit was touted by the news media as a blank slate where anyone could move to pursue dreams and goals not attainable elsewhere. This narrative promoted an influx of a young, White population, overlooking the struggles of older, predominantly African American residents, already living on fixed incomes, reduced services, and uncertain futures. Real estate developers showcased Detroit as the 'Comeback City', pointing to renovated downtown buildings, rendering invisible the lives of thousands of low-income seniors living in Department of Housing and Urban Development (HUD) Project-Based Section 8 Housing (a housing voucher system).

Seniors reside in varied housing in the city, ranging from single-family homes in depopulated neighborhoods to high-rise buildings in downtown and midtown. Pressure to preserve housing for seniors in the city is great because when Section 8 building contracts expire, there is the possibility of managers transferring vouchers to other buildings. This displaces communities of tenants by moving them to other buildings accepting individualized housing vouchers throughout the city. In addition, rent increases are forcing residents to make different housing choices in less centralized areas. As urban communities plan for the reopening of the economy, the impact on seniors' living arrangements remains unknown, as commercial real estate in the same spaces may affect pressures on senior buildings in the greater downtown area. This could displace even more residents with few alternative housing options available to them. Project-based buildings serve an extremely low income (ELI) renter, often bringing in only 20 percent of the city's Area Median Income (AMI), who do not qualify for most of the publicized 'affordable housing' options (Perry et al,

2020). We advocate in this chapter that the heterogeneity of the senior housing landscape, as well as of older adults themselves, needs to be understood in order to address their concerns and support their resilience.

The intersection of race and spatial inequity: rights denied in Detroit's housing history

Housing is not a new issue for Detroit. At the height of World War II, Detroit faced a massive housing shortage. New Black families, fleeing deadly Klu Klux Klan terrorism in the Jim Crow South and looking for greater opportunity in the North, arrived every day.[2] Racial prejudice was pervasive in the North also, making economic opportunities for Black families hard fought. Many neighborhoods imposed strict, Whites-only racial covenants, tightly controlling which families could move into an area. In 1941, Detroit designated 12 housing sites for Black workers. The most prominent were the Sojourner Truth Homes, located on the city's east side. Nearby White residents, infuriated at Sojourner Truth's construction, demanded it be reserved for Whites; KKK-led mobs assaulted the site's first Black residents as they moved into their new homes.

In 1943, race and housing contributed to greater unrest; in 1967, Detroiters again fought with police fueled by housing discrimination, inadequate social services, and racist police practices. The federal government established the Kerner Commission to investigate the causes of the unrest, which reported that White-led de facto segregation provided the main cause for the uprising. The commission reported that, unless drastic changes were made addressing housing discrimination and economic opportunity, existing disparities would only widen, and that America would move 'toward two societies, one black, one white – separate and unequal' (1968). Instead of heeding the Commission's warning, local and state governments doubled down with budget increases for policing and prisons, sacrificing spending on education, social services, and community engagement. Detroiters faced higher unemployment, reduced access to healthy food and medicine, inadequate infrastructure, and greater disparities in health care. White residents relocated to suburban communities, but decades-old legacies of redlining and racist lending practices reinforced barriers that kept many Black families from leaving.

As the city's financial situation worsened, aging Detroiters faced water shutoffs, reduced transportation access, tax foreclosures, and evictions. As older Detroiters aged out of their homes, or lost them to foreclosure, many had to seek HUD housing. HUD provided downtown apartment owners with subsidies to guarantee full occupancy in exchange for providing affordable housing units for a duration of 20 to 30 years. Recently, some of Detroit's Project-based Section 8 housing contracts have expired, and more expirations are on the horizon.

The pandemic leaves Detroit's most vulnerable populations isolated in senior apartments

> The company that owned the building wouldn't supply us with masks. Only management had masks, management and maintenance workers. The rest of the building, they could care less. (Cynthia West)

SHP-D's work in advocating for senior housing preservation to ensure 'One Detroit for All' has always constituted the core of its activities. However, amid the COVID-19 pandemic, the immediate health needs of seniors living in congregate housing has expanded, thus reiterating the importance of the link between stable housing and the health and well-being of seniors. Initially, Michigan's governor required COVID-19 testing for nursing homes, but residents at low-income senior housing buildings were left out. While managers of some non-profit buildings offered greater support to their residents, other low-income senior buildings did not. Amid the pandemic, SHP-D's advocacy and outreach to municipal departments contributed to the Mayor of Detroit, Mike Duggan, offering free COVID-19 testing to those aged 60 and older. Prescription requirements for testing were waived and the Detroit Health Department began offering testing at senior buildings where, catastrophically, 87 percent of senior buildings yielded positive tests (Frank, 2020).

Detroit accounts for approximately 24 percent of all fatalities in the state, despite representing only 6 percent of the state's total population; 81.8 percent were Detroiters aged 60 or older. While Governor Whitmer reinstated water service for 3,000 Detroiters, the state's eviction moratorium (expired July 1, 2020) and Detroit's August 15 extension. Though there have been subsequent extensions to this moratorium, local moratoriams and the national CDC declarations have proven to be a stopgap measure (Rahman, 2020). Detroiters' well-being has also been subject to a backdrop of mixed national messaging, which contributes to disease resurgences and compromises Americans' ability to flatten the curve, much less address the impact on older and minority populations with decades of inequitable access to health care. In a city with one of the worst regional transit system in the nation, persistent classifications of Detroit as a food desert, and the elimination of the municipal office dedicated to senior services, meeting the needs of vulnerable seniors necessitated a strategic shift by SHP-D (Archambault et al, 2020).

Going forward: ensuring health and housing for older Detroiters

Everyone was scared to death, literally. Nobody knew what was going on in the world. It hit us personally. We

were afraid to go outside. We didn't know what we could
or could not do. They hadn't established the proper social
distancing and wearing the mask. (George West)

As chapters throughout this series demonstrate, the pandemic is
inherently linked to issues of economic and social justice. Older
adults – particularly those of color – disproportionately suffer
from the effects of the virus; *this stems from disparities not only in
fields of economic opportunity and health care, but from spatial disparities associated with housing, as well.* Reliable and safe housing, in
conjunction with education and support from property management and service coordinators, are essential to preventing
the virus's spread (see Tunstall, Chapter Two; Xavier, Chapter
Seven; Brown et al, Chapter Ten). As we anticipate the duration of the pandemic, intersections of the annual flu and
COVID-19, as well as combating fatigue of social distance and
health precautions, it is imperative that stakeholders maintain
their communication and share resources.

In the past, SHP-D has taken proactive steps to contribute
to research and policies on how issues relating to housing specifically affect seniors' health. SHP-D's relocation assessment
tool (found in Perry et al, 2020), health and housing assessment
(in development) and support of the Notification Ordinance
passed by Detroit's City Council in 2017 represents the
coalition's pioneering efforts to raise awareness on how stressors
related to housing negatively affect health. This includes not
only physical health, but mental and spiritual well-being also:

Housing insecurity is a critical determinant of health.
Living with the potential of eviction or foreclosure, or
experiencing homelessness creates toxic stress, [which]
may complicate disease management, and undercuts
health maintenance. Living in unsafe and unhealthy
environments also helps determine poor health. (Perry
et al, 2020)

Some American policy proposals have been put forward that would provide seniors and other low-income households with greater security, such as universal housing vouchers; these would extend Section 8 housing vouchers to all who qualify, replacing the current approach of fund allocation. This approach could transform the affordable housing landscape and avert many who revolve between being precariously housed and being homeless into more predictable life courses (Cunningham, 2020). Other efforts to preserve housing affordability have been focused on American cities creating trust funds for affordable housing supported by special millages, or designated income streams. Another mechanism has been to offer current residents the right of first refusal of their residences, which allows them to buy them, or to transfer the right to buy to non-profit developers.

These important approaches to preserving housing often involve numerous partnerships between city government, non-profits as well as regional and national initiatives. A coalition such as SHP-D, has a strong role to play in these advocacy efforts. SHP-D's current strategic plan has three major directions: 1) understanding the changing context; 2) making connections; and 3) advocacy (see Perry et al, 2020). The community-based work of coalitions may become even more important as the affordable housing crisis overtakes many urban spaces.

Given the predicted demographic shifts, the crucial need to expand housing options for older adults and allow people to keep their communities intact must continue to be advocated for in this country. SHP-D will continue in its essential work, crucial in the campaign for seniors' access to low-income housing in Detroit. Amid one of the worst pandemics the globe has seen in a century, and with a growing senior population that has been likened to a coming 'silver tsunami', the link between housing and health has never been more pressing.

Notes

[1] The names/identifying information of older Detroiters quoted in this chapter have been altered to protect their privacy. All quotes are from interviews with HUD Section 8 housing residents in the greater downtown Detroit area.

[2] The Jim Crow South refers to discriminatory policies that legalized racial segregation and denial of key liberties. For more information, see Chafe et al (2011).

References

Archambault, D., Sanford, S. and Perry, T. (2020) 'Detroit's efforts to meet the needs of seniors: macro responses to a crisis'. *Journal of Gerontological Social Work*, https://doi.org/10.1080/01634372.2020.1797974

Chafe, W.H., Gavins, R. and Korstad, R. (eds) (2011) *Remembering Jim Crow: African Americans Tell About Life in the Segregated South*. New York: The New Press.

Cunningham, M. (2020) 'It's time to reinforce the housing safety net by adopting universal vouchers for low-income renters'. *Housing and Housing Finance blog*. Washington: Urban Institute. Retrieved from: www.urban.org/urban-wire/its-time-reinforce-housing-safety-net-adopting-universal-vouchers-low-income-renters

Detroit Health Department (2020) *COVID-19 Dashboard, 2020*. https://codtableau.detroitmi.gov/t/DHD/views/CityofDetroit-PublicCOVIDDashboard/DemographicCasesDashboard

Frank, A. (2020) 'In Detroit findings so far, 87 percent of senior apartment facilities have COVID-19 cases'. *Crain's*, May 11.

Kerner Commission (1968) *Report of the National Advisory Commission on civil disorders*. Washington: United States, Kerner Commission: U.S. G.P.O.

Perry, T.E., Archambault, D. and Sanford, C.S. (2017) 'Preserving senior housing in a changing city: innovative efforts of an interprofessional coalition'. *Public Policy & Aging Report*, 27 (Suppl. 1, December 29) pp S22–S26.

Perry, T.E., Wintermute, T., Carney, B.C., Leach, D.E., Sanford, C. and Quist, L.E. (2015) 'Senior housing at a crossroads: a case study of a university/community partnership in Detroit, Michigan'. *Traumatology*, 21(3): 244–50, DOI: 10.1037/trm0000043

Perry, T.E., Berglund, L., Mah, J., Sanford, C., Schaeffer, P. and Villeneuve, E.W. (2020) 'Advocating for the preservation of senior housing: a coalition at work amidst gentrification in Detroit, Michigan'. *Housing Policy Debate*, 1–120, https://doi.org/10.10 80/10511482.2020.1806899

Rahman, N. (2020) 'CDC eviction ban: what tenants should know about new guidance from the state, Detroit court'. *Detroit Free Press*, September 4.

Rorai, V. and T. Perry. (2020) 'An innovative telephone outreach program to seniors in Detroit, a city facing dire consequences of COVID-19'. *Journal of Gerontological Social Work*, 63(6–7): 713–16, https://doi.org/10.1080/01634372.2020.1793254

FOURTEEN

Ethnic Enclaves in a Time of Plague: A Comparative Analysis of New York City and Chicago

Amanda Furiasse and Sher Afgan Tareen

As the first wave of the COVID-19 pandemic peaked in the late spring of 2020 in the United States, the strategy for mitigating the spread of the virus centered around limiting bodily interactions between people, known popularly as 'social distancing'. Mayors across US cities delegated the task of monitoring social distancing to the local police. As soon as local police began to execute the new public health mandates, racial minorities were 80 percent more likely to be ticketed and issued summons for social distancing violations (Moore, 2020).

This chapter examines why social distancing mandates are enforced disproportionately on racial minorities by offering a comparative analysis of Williamsburg, Brooklyn, and Englewood, Chicago. Both of these urban neighborhoods have historically allowed racial and religious minorities to configure a home that exceeds beyond an apartment or other legally classified residential dwelling to include a broad range of built structures such as schools, delis, synagogues, churches, and parks. However, digital technologies, such as iPhone tracking devices and iPhone apps, that allow users to report violators of social distancing have rendered such private spaces as contagious, thus emboldening public officials to regulate them as part of policing social distancing. This central tension not only exacerbates the contentious relationship between state officials and minorities but also reverses state officials' historical approach to the maintenance and regulation of public health in US cities. Far from a legal or political theory, we argue that the idea of the 'private' structures the urban design of New York City and Chicago into discrete neighborhoods, protecting religious and racial minorities from persistent surveillance, and must be maintained through the production of urban spaces which facilitate religious and racial minorities to move around without constant surveillance (see also Volume 3).

Germ theory and the ethnic enclave

Measures taken against the spread of infectious diseases for at least two centuries have played a formative role in urban design. In particular, industrializing cities during the turn of the 20th century were compartmentalized into discrete ethnic neighborhoods that were set apart from public spaces of gathering to restrict the mobility of incoming migrants who were feared to have been carriers of deadly epidemics. In the aftermath of the tuberculosis epidemic, nativists mobilized scientific discoveries in virology and epidemiology, called germ theory, to affix tuberculosis (TB) onto Jewish migrants arriving at Ellis Island (Markel, 1999: 5). Presumed carriers of tuberculosis were held in indefinite quarantines or sent back to their home countries, with little regard for separating them from family members who accompanied them on the long journey (Markel, 1999: 26). Those who succeeded at entering the city were nonetheless contained within neighborhoods which naturalized association between Jewishness and tuberculosis. For instance, the Lower East Side was named the 'lung district' in reference to the lungs of the poverty-stricken children of the Jewish migrants suffering from tuberculosis (Wenger, 1999: 84).

In January 1934, the state of New York passed the Municipal Housing Authorities Law that mandated city officials inspect homes and demolish the ones that failed to abide by certain public health requirements such as basic ventilation standards (Karlin, 1937). The law reflected a shift in the understanding of infectious diseases as spread by structural inequities in housing, labor, and access to health care (Goetz, 2013: 25). Contradictorily, state officials treated Jewish communities as victims of structural inequality while simultaneously enacting policies which stripped them of their housing rights (Mendelsohn, 2009: 24).

By mid-century, opportunities arose for Jews to relocate elsewhere. In particular, the Williamsburg neighborhood in Brooklyn promised the revival of a new ethnic enclave anchored around Orthodox Jews who had recently fled Nazi persecution and aspired for privacy as key to their survival (Mayer, 1979: 33; Kranzler, 1995). Orthodox Jewish communities in Williamsburg created public health programs which partner with local synagogues to provide testing for genetic diseases and share information on early detection (Kranzler, 1995: 252–3). Such initiatives were precipitated by the federal government's classification of Orthodox Jews as a disadvantaged minority. Once contained within Williamsburg, they were no longer deemed a threat to public health, afflicted by illnesses that could potentially infect a non-Jew.

The association between germs and racial minorities which galvanized public health campaigns to contain New York's Jewish migrants within discrete ethnic neighborhoods in the midst of the TB epidemic led to similar initiatives in Chicago for containing influenza in the 'Black Belt', a region in the southwestern part of the city between Wentworth Avenue and Cottage Grove Avenue reserved exclusively for the city's Black tenants. In the aftermath of the influenza epidemic, incoming

African American migrants from the rural south were blamed for the spread of the disease in Chicago even though the earliest casualties were predominantly White. The exclusive scrutiny over the incoming African American migrants was informed by fears that they lacked knowledge of hygiene and cleanliness due to the absence of institutionalized health care facilities in the rural south (Schlabach, 2019: 37). Ironically, most of the hospitals in Chicago barred Black patients from entering the facility. The assumption that racial mixing was the source of influenza led to a series of preventative measures in homes, streets, salons, and dance halls as well that delineated certain blocks of streets in Chicago as White and other blocks as Black.

These measures included making home visitations in residences west of Cottage Grove Avenue which included the neighborhood of Englewood. Once cherished as hideouts from urban vice and pollution, Englewood's households transformed into dangerous hot spots for influenza made visible by the red placards that nurses placed on the front door to designate the property as diseased (Schlabach, 2019: 43). Even children playing on the streets outside were subjected to medical inspections and dispersed if suspected of carrying symptoms for influenza (Schlabach, 2019: 42). While reducing play time for Englewood's Black youth, such home visitations also allayed anxieties about the spread of influenza into residential blocks east of Cottage Grove Avenue which had been delineated as exclusively White. As examples of infectious diseases associated with the bodies of African American and Jewish working migrants, influenza and TB gave rise to distinct urban neighborhoods of Englewood and Williamsburg where privacy is constituted by the absence of mobility.

Policing social distancing in the enclave

In the midst of the COVID-19 pandemic, social media, such as Twitter, threaten to dissolve the privacy of racial minorities by turning their private gatherings within ethnic enclaves into violations of public health mandates (Hess, 2020). A house party in southwest Chicago, for instance, was spotlighted on Twitter, arousing scathing criticisms from all kinds of users including Chicago's mayor, Lori Lightfoot. Mayor Lightfoot condemned the gathering and tweeted in response that all Chicagoans must follow social distancing guidelines (Torres, 2020), yet the Chicago Police were only dispatched to the region's predominantly Black residences. A month later, the Chicago Police dispersed a crowd gathering in Englewood (D'Onofrio and Jordan, 2020). Mayor Lightfoot's tweet in response depicted the incident as one about the failure of the local residents of Englewood to abide by stay-at-home order (D'Onofrio and Jordan, 2020). Twitter has also empowered New York City's mayor Bill DeBlasio to publicize the ritual practices of Jews living in Williamsburg in order to absolve the city for its struggles at containing the spread of the COVID-19. After videos of mourners gathered at the funeral of a prominent rabbi appeared on Twitter and Instagram, Mayor DeBlasio wrote a tweet promising mass arrest of any Orthodox Jewish person who violated the city's social distancing regulations (Stack, 2020). His exclusive focus on Orthodox Jewish communities as violators of social distancing received backlash from the Anti-Defamation League. In its complaint, the Anti-Defamation League reminded the public that 'while there certainly have been several isolated instances of non-compliance, these aberrations are not unique to the Haredi or Orthodox communities' (Anti-Defamation League, 2020). Similarly, New York City public advocate Jumaane Williams drew attention to variations in social distancing's enforcement in US cities and brought attention to the unwillingness of police departments to release public information about how they were enforcing social distancing and public health interventions in different communities (Williams, 2020).

While public advocates and activists correctly predicted that the policing of social distancing would inevitably lead to the targeting of neighborhoods such as Williamsburg and Englewood that have a large concentration of minority residents, they failed to foresee the extent to which digital surveillance technologies would render the bodies of Williamsburg and Englewood's residents into dangerous leaks of contagion. In effect, government officials approached their embodied actions as dangerous and contagious in that somehow a private family funeral between Jewish families or family parties would spill out into the streets of Manhattan, infecting all of New York City residents. Put differently, government officials assumed that the images and sounds mediated to them by their phones and computers were themselves contagious or mediating an unfiltered material reality which could infect their bodies in the same way COVID-19 could infect them.

Government officials' understanding of events in effect flipped the dichotomy of the public/private distinction on its head and rendered the subjects gathered at private events into public spectacles. Residents at private events were outed as acting publicly in private or as Wendy Chun describes it 'caught in public acting privately' (Chun, 2017: 95). Sounds and images on Twitter consequently broke down the physical walls and boundaries separating a private event between family and friends from government officials. Government officials in turn portrayed these private gatherings as if they were somehow occurring in the homes and living rooms of residents throughout the city. This breakdown between the public/private dichotomy rendered the digital images and sounds of people privately gathered together as if they were in fact contagious and jeopardizing the physical, material health, and safety of others. As fears of contagion converged with digital technologies, a common theme became redolent across media platforms: urban neighborhoods, otherwise rendered invisible by zoning, suddenly transformed into global media spectacles of contagion. Moreover, these social media posts converged around religious and racial minorities who inhabited these otherwise invisible neighborhoods.

Digital technologies' convergence around religious and racial minorities raises important questions about technology's role and influence on public health's application. Put simply, why are social media users converging around religious and racial minorities who live in ethnic enclaves? Moreover, how are digital technologies reshaping and influencing people's understanding of disease and health in US cities? While the neighborhoods of Williamsburg, NY and Englewood, Chicago have emerged into public spectacles of contagion on Twitter, they were historically concealed from the public by emerging theories in biomedicine, especially germ theory, that sought to arrest the spread of contagious diseases from the city's working migrants to its White residents.

Conclusion

Germ theory and fears of infectious disease informed state officials' approach to the design of US cities and repositioned racial and religious minorities into discrete enclaves to mitigate the spread of contagious diseases. The concept of privacy thus structured the basic design of US cities with the enclave emerging as a result of the convergence of innovations in science, urban planning, and public health. With the advent of digital technologies, this spatial ordering of privacy is increasingly unraveling as social media and phone apps allow people to enter spaces once deemed private. This shift represents a reversal or inversion of state officials' mitigation techniques in the past when they instituted the spatial delineation of the private to cloister racial and religious minorities into enclaves, set apart from space deemed public. The growing fear of the ubiquitous spread of contagious diseases in the present moment raises a pressing question for urban planners: how should the ethnic enclaves be designed to protect the privacy of racial minorities who are disproportionately targeted for public health guideline infractions? The digital space both creates conditions for users to abrogate the privacy of racial minorities yet also offers a lens for designing built environments that restore it. Modeled after the private chat rooms on social media apps such as Facebook, we propose that urban planners design ethnic enclaves as a series of high-walled enclosures. Doing so would maximize feelings of intimacy and togetherness yet also rebuffing the capacity of digital technologies to jeopardize the safety and security of the local community.

References

Anti-Defamation League (2020) *On Social Media, Haredi and Orthodox Jewish Communities are Scapegoated and Blamed for COVID-19*, April 29, www.adl.org/blog/on-social-media-haredi-and-orthodox-jewish-communities-are-scapegoated-and-blamed-for-COVID-19

Chun, W.H.K. (2017) *Updating to Remain the Same: Habitual New Media*. Boston: MIT Press.

D'Onofrio, J. and Jordan, K. (2020) *Chicago police address stay-at-home order enforcement after video shows scuffle with crowd in Englewood*. ABC7, May 26, https://abc7chicago.com/chicago-police-englewood-lori-lightfoot-chance-the-rapper/6212076/

Goetz, E.G. (2013) *New Deal Ruins: Race, Economic Justice, and Public Housing Policy*. Ithaca, NY: Cornell University Press.

Hess, A, (2020) 'The social-distancing shamers are watching'. *The New York Times*, May 11, www.nytimes.com/2020/05/11/arts/social-distance-shaming.html

Karlin, W. (1937) 'New York slum clearance and the law'. *Political Science Quarterly*, 52(2): 241–58.

Kranzler, G. (1995) *Hasidic Williamsburg: A Contemporary American Hasidic Community*. Lanham, MD: Jason Aronson, Incorporated.

Markel, H. (1999) *Quarantine!: East European Jewish Immigrants and the New York City Epidemics of 1892*. Baltimore: Johns Hopkins University Press.

Mayer, E. (1979) *From Suburb to Shtetl: The Jews of Boro Park*. Philadelphia: Temple University Press.

Mendelsohn, J. (2009) *The Lower East Side Remembered and Revisited: A History and Guide to a Legendary New York Neighborhood*. New York: Columbia University Press.

Moore, T. (2020) *NYPD union wants cops out of 'social distancing enforcement'*. New York Post Blog, May 4, nypost.com/2020/05/04/nypd-union-wants-cops-out-of-social-distancing-enforcement/

Schlabach, E. (2019) 'The influenza epidemic and the Jim Crow public health policies and practices in Chicago, 1917–1921'. *The Journal of African American History*, 104(1): 31–58.

Stack, L. (2020) 'De blasio breaks up rabbi's funeral and lashes out over virus distancing'. *The New York Times*, April 28, www.nytimes.com/2020/04/28/nyregion/hasidic-funeral-coronavirus-de-blasio.html

Torres, S. (2020) *Mayor Lightfoot condemns large house party reportedly in Chicago*. NBC5, April 27, www.nbcchicago.com/news/local/mayor-lightfoot-condemns-large-house-party-reportedly-in-chicago/2262179/

Wenger, B.S. (1999) *New York Jews and Great Depression: Uncertain Promise*. Syracuse, NY: Syracuse University Press.

Williams, J.D. (2020) *NYC public advocate's statement on social distancing enforcement arrests and inequities*. Office of the New York City Public Advocate, May 4, https://advocate.nyc.gov/press/nyc-public-advocates-statement-social-distancing-enforcement-arrests-and-inequities/

FIFTEEN

Migration in the Times of Immobility: Liminal Geographies of Walking and Dispossession in India

Kamalika Banerjee and Samadrita Das

This chapter engages with liminality in a state of exception in the context of the pandemic-induced lockdown in India which displaced thousands of migrants from the urban nerve centers of the country. While the lockdown imposed a nationwide state of exception which restricted mobility, suspended fundamental rights of participating in the public life, and reduced human life to bare life (Agamben, 2020; Nagesh et al, Volume 1), the migrant laborers in India, who mostly work in big cities under precarious living conditions, inhabited a state of both social and spatial liminality. In the wake of the national lockdown, which came into effect on March 25, 2020, thousands of laborers who originally hailed from the hinterlands of non-industrial states, started walking back to their villages from the industrial cities after losing their jobs and therefore the ability to afford to stay in the city. Our focus in this chapter is to understand liminality in the state of exception for the urban poor, marked by their 'dwelling in displacement' (Saxena, 2020), where they found themselves 'stuck in the interstices of material and discursive spaces, leaving them with lingering precarity' (Saxena, 2020: 2). Bhan et al (2020) point out how Southern responses to, and experiences of the pandemic are vastly different from the Northern processes; practices such as social distancing and working from home are especially difficult to observe, especially for the subaltern (see also Lemanski and De Groot, Volume 1). In this sense, the pandemic ceases to be a portal, as exhorted by Roy (2020) in her provocative *Financial Times* article, where the '"before" and "after" of the pandemic, and where the "crisis" and the "everyday" are not so neatly separable' but 'continued in intensified contingencies' and compounded precarity and risks (Bhan et al, 2020). Our chapter attempts to understand the splintered and fragmented nature of pandemic governance, the lockdown and state of exception, instead of thinking in terms of totality.

Images of migrant laborers – young and old, pregnant women, children, and the elderly – on the news and social media haunted the nation with memories of the partition of India in 1947 (Biswas, 2020) and the Bengal famine of 1943 (Dutta, 2020). The pandemic-related migration was not triggered by a political crisis but it translated into a political predicament. The inefficiency or apathy of the state and the shifting of the onus to the poor laborers, blurs the boundary between migrants and refugees and opens the ingress to a Southern way of COVID-19 management. While many of the migrants died from exhaustion, accidents, and starvation, the state took little responsibility in alleviating the crisis. The displacement of migrants from their homes and their liminality during the lockdown triggered various forms of dispossession and precarity.

The lockdown and the urban poor

As COVID-19 spread around the world in the beginning of 2020, urban societies, as nodes of international connection, concentration of economic activities, and public life, came to a standstill in order to contain the spread of the virus. Consequently, most countries around the world imposed lockdowns and suspended a host of economic activities, rules which were heavily monitored by governments. In India, a countrywide lockdown was enforced on March 25, 2020 (Gettleman and Schultz, 2020). This triggered an acute dilemma for the contract laborers, street vendors, factory workers, and other informal sector laborers, who had migrated from either the hinterlands of states to the big cities, or from poorer states such as Uttar Pradesh and West Bengal to work in more affluent cities and states in Southern India, like Mumbai, Hyderabad, Bangalore, and in various sectors in Kerala. With the suspension of transport infrastructures in the weeks that followed the lockdown order, these migrant workers started walking across city and state borders to go back to their villages of origin.

The mass exodus from cities involved men, women, children, and the elderly embarking on journeys of thousands of kilometers on foot, by bicycle, on the back of trucks, vans, and other means to reach their native villages. The spectacle of walking migrants exposed the invisible population of these workers, hitherto unseen because of their ambivalent status as seasonal unregistered workers. Not everyone made it back; many died on the way, run over by vehicles, by goods-trains (Banerjee and Mahale, 2020), or died from severe exhaustion.

The state stood as a mere spectator to it all. On March 28 2020, innumerable migrant workers gathered at New Delhi's Anand Vihar Interstate Bus Terminus, violating all state-ordained decrees of social distancing and other precautionary measures, to return to their native villages (Singh, 2020). After receiving pressure from state governments, the Union government allowed trains to transport migrant laborers to their respective states. However, despite demands for a subsidy, the central government evaded paying train fares for poor migrants (The Wire Analysis, 2020). Additionally, in the Monsoon

Session of the Parliament, held in September 2020, in response to queries from the opposition, the Union government revealed that it did not have any data regarding the number of job losses and laborer deaths for the period of the lockdown (Nath, 2020). However, an RTI report filed by The Wire reveals that the government deliberately withheld this data (Mishra, 2020). The RTI application was filed from 18 zones of the Indian Railways and revealed that at least 80 people died on special trains transporting migrant workers home (Mishra, 2020). Also, a group of independent researchers, who collated data from newspapers and online portals on non-virus deaths (Mishra, 2020) reported that at least 971 people died from exhaustion, financial distress, and road accidents.

The absence of the state in handling the migrant-laborer crisis during the pandemic-induced lockdown reveals not only the everyday dispossession and vulnerability of the urban poor, even in non-crisis situations, but also unveils the everyday failure and inefficiency of the postcolonial state in India. The state, in this context, in contradistinction to the idea of the totalitarian biopolitical state, is governed more by electoral interests, where several states like West Bengal (*The Hindu*), consistently fudged data related to COVID-19 infections and deaths, in the face of the upcoming elections in 2021. In response to this gap in governance, civil society helped the migrant laborers and the urban poor in a variety of ways. Bollywood film star Sonu Sood, as part of his *Ghar Bhejo* (home bound) campaign, helped 12,000 migrants to reach home (by May 27, 2020) and was preparing for another 45,000 workers to be sent home, reported by Dundoo (2020) for *The Hindu*. Even ordinary citizens stepped in to crowdfund resources through social media platforms to provide food and other essential goods to stranded laborers in the cities and in the liminal spaces, to the walking workers, operating from living rooms and college common rooms (Gupta et al, 2020). The Supreme Court of India appreciated the efforts of the NGOs in providing for the displaced laborers (Press Trust of India, 2020).

The pandemic-induced lockdown not only created liminal spaces of walking and dispossession for the urban poor, but also exposed the liminal space or critical gaps in state governance, which is often filled by the civil society in India. The spread of COVID-19 in India not only demonstrated the urban poor's concern for their right to the city, but also their right to return. While the elite carriers of the disease from foreign destinations were brought back home on chartered planes, sometimes free of charge (The Wire Analysis, 2020), poor laborers were neither provided with transportation support and safe accommodation facilities in the host cities nor monetary compensation for retrenchment and non-payment of remuneration by contractors (Varma, 2020). In the absence of the state, vast tracts of anarchic liminal spaces were formed (see also Bal et al, Volume 1).

Geographies of liminality during a state of exception

The concept of liminality encompasses issues of 'unboundedness, spillage, fluidity, multiplicity, and processes of contingent, non-linear becoming...' (March, 2020: 1). March delineates that in terms of space, liminality can explain 'interstices, gaps and voids... with passageways... borders and questions of permeability... and with vagueness' (March, 2020: 2). The Chicago school has used liminality to designate the disorganized and deviant spaces, in contradistinction to the more organized spaces of the city (March, 2020). As unplanned spaces, such landscapes are both marginalized and subversive, scripting both violence against its occupants and users, as well as enabling insurgency and occupancy, allowing the subaltern to claim and use such spaces tactically.

The roads, highways, railway tracks, and detours through the wilderness became liminal spaces in the first few weeks of the lockdown, when migrant laborers lost their sources of income in big cities and started journeying back to their native villages. In an ironic breach of decree, where citizens' mobilities were severely restricted and the state mandated staying indoors, the liminal citizens (in a sense that their citizenship was suspended because of their status as being-in-transit) thronged in-between spaces and posited a form of transgressive behavior, albeit forced. The United Nations High Commissioner for Refugees (UNHCR) makes an important distinction between a migrant and a refugee in terms of choice (Edwards, 2016); while the refugee is fleeing persecution, the migrant moves voluntarily in search of better employment, and unlike refugees, migrants can safely return home and continue to be protected by the home government. The migrant crisis in India shatters the myth of this distinction. The precarious liminal spaces, where people died or were killed in accidents, highlights the refugee-predicament of the migrant laborers, forced to flee and unattended to by the state.

It is also imperative to mention that the centralized nature of the Indian state came to assume a quasi-Federal spirit in handling inter-state migration during lockdown. This is evinced in the fact that migrant laborers were first put in overcrowded shelter homes and 'quarantine jails' to limit their movement across state borders (Ghosh and Basu Ray Chaudhury, 2020). Subsequently, host states like Kerala undertook institutional and infrastructural measures, like designating them as 'guest workers' and serving customized cuisine catering to the workers' palate, to deter them from traveling (Arnimesh, 2020). The most dehumanizing act that captured national attention was when migrant laborers were sprayed with disinfectant at the Uttar Pradesh border, to cleanse them before allowing entry inside the state. The withdrawal of the state from the liminal spaces is pronounced in its imposition and surveillance in the governed spaces. While it is an oversimplification to state that the government is only protecting its elite citizens, as COVID-19 management in India has been haphazard and incremental, the worst sufferers have been migrant laborers. Therefore, it is important to note that an analysis of COVID-19 management in Indian (and other Southern) cities is best understood in its fragments, in the liminal spaces of governance, geography, and society, where the state of exception is suspended, lockdown-related laws are violated with legal impunity and different segments of society are subject to diverse forms of biopolitics.

The migrant worker, even in everyday urban life, is suspended between being an illegitimate encroacher in the host city and serving as a pool of necessary and cheap labor (Ghosh and Basu Ray Chaudhury, 2020; Qamhaieh, Volume 1). History has witnessed mass exoduses of laborers from cities in the face of plagues and natural calamities: in 1896, workers fled the city after a bubonic plague in the working-class settlements in colonial Bombay killed many workers (Rao, 2013), the 1994 plague in Western India spurred the exodus of thousands of people from Surat, in Gujarat, and many workers fled Mumbai in the aftermath of the 2005 floods (Biswas, 2020). This is because the life of the migrant worker is perennially suspended in liminality, threatened by eviction drives by the state, destroyed by natural calamities such as floods and cyclones, and imperiled by a lack of adequate social securities (stemming from their status as non-registered contractual workers or street vendors, and so on).

There is a litany of labor laws in place to safeguard labor rights like the Inter-State Migrant Workmen (Regulation of Employment and Conditions of Service) Act, 1979 and the simplified Occupational Safety, Health and Working Conditions Code created in 2019, which incorporates 13 labor laws (including the Act of 1979) (Varma, 2020). However, as with most other laws in India, these regulations remain unenforced, creating fault lines of socio-spatial and political precarities for migrant laborers. Also, because of their transitory status, torn between the host and the home states, migrant laborers are often left out of the electoral system, thereby being denied their fundamental citizenship rights (Varma, 2020).

The COVID-19 crisis exacerbated the pre-existing vulnerabilities of migrant workers (see Bal et al; Azlan; Chattoraj; Qamhaieh; Yea, all Volume 1). We argue that the liminal spaces between cities and places are spatialized productions of their pre-existing liminality, generated in the everyday experiences of precarious living and working in the cities. While under normal circumstances, the liminal spaces of their dwelling often accord them agency, through tactical occupation (Benjamin, 2008), by manipulating the corrupt state system through 'illicit dealings with low-level state functionaries' (Anjaria, 2011: 58), in a state of exception, when the state apparatus is unsettled and the migrants lose their source of income, their dwelling is displaced. The subaltern tactics of occupation are oriented to legal loopholes. In a state of exception, when the juridical order is suspended, such tactics become anarchic, like gathering at bus and railway terminuses, based on rumors and hearsay, only to be lathi-charged and dispersed by the police (Dahat and Jain, 2020). Nevertheless, the tactics of walking or crowdsourcing vans to go back, highlight the violence of the state, in its withdrawal and suspension. Unlike a slum demolition or hawker eviction, where the subaltern can approach the court or bribe officials, in the state of exception, 'bare life reaches its maximum indeterminacy' (Agamben, 2005: 4) Therefore, we argue that the Indian state did not impose draconian measures unlike other states in the world, especially in these liminal spaces. Instead, the state withdrew from these interstitial spaces, occupied by the liminal migrant workers, and evaded the politics of both 'duty' and 'care'.

Conclusion

Southern urban crises often witness state apathy and ineptitude rather than totalitarianism, because of the fragmented nature of the state and the society (Bhan et al, 2020). Through an analysis of the liminal spaces in the state of exception of the lockdown, which generated new forms of dispossession and vulnerability for the migrant laborers, we present a case of a fragmented state of exception. In this scenario, instead of unleashing direct violence on the population, the state withdraws from certain political and geographical landscapes to create a refugee crisis. The paradoxical mass mobility triggered by a lockdown that decreed immobility augmented the pre-existing vulnerabilities of migrant laborers in India.

Scholarship on the Indian state reveals how it functions through provisional mechanisms, ridden by corruption and characterized by inefficiency and ineptitude (Anjaria, 2011). Therefore, the withdrawal of the state during the COVID-19 pandemic followed the pre-existing script of the politics of absence. Like everyday urban management, where civil society has come to be the new guardians of cities (Ghertner, 2011), civil society filled the political vacuum, through disparate acts of charity and entrepreneurialism, further legitimizing the state's inaction. In this context, Kerala's response to the crisis, in terms of working with the migrants, ensuring their physical and emotional well-being, is an important model for other states and the Center to follow (Arnimesh, 2020). In this chapter, our analysis leaves the physical boundary of the city with the migrant workers and pushes the frontiers of the politics of displacement and dwelling in liminality by highlighting that urban policy should not only be attuned to housing and the rights of the urban poor in the city, but also needs to address the right to return, and to dwell, in times of crisis and emergency.

References

Agamben, G. (2005) *State of Exception* (translated by Kevin Attell). Chicago: University of Chicago Press.

Agamben, G. (2020) 'Clarifications'. Retrieved from: https://itself. blog/2020/03/17/giorgio-agamben-clarifications/?fbclid=IwA R3y8hIOkUIFgxfITZ4qVxNmhLyHfa2y7QE2rm7dJOLNPp WVNkEjrfFiMr4

Anjaria, J.S. (2011) 'Ordinary states: everyday corruption and the politics of space in Mumbai'. *American Ethnologist*, https://doi. org/10.1111/j.1548-1425.2010.01292.x

Arnimesh, S. (2020) 'Rotis, mobile recharges, carrom boards: how Kerala fixed its migrant worker anger'. *The Print*, April 18. Retrieved from: https://theprint.in/india/rotis-mobile-recharges-carrom-boards-how-kerala-fixed-its-migrant-worker-anger/403937/

Banerjee, S. and Mahale, A. (2020) '16 migrant workers run over by goods train near Aurangabad in Maharashtra'. *The Hindu*, May 8. Retrieved from: www.thehindu.com/news/national/other-states/16-migrant-workers-run-over-by-goods-train-near-aurangabad-in-maharashtra/article31531352.ece

Benjamin, S. (2008) 'Occupancy urbanism: radicalizing politics and economy beyond policy and programs'. *International Journal of Urban and Regional Research*, 32(3): 719–29, https://doi.org/10.1111/j.1468-2427.2008.00809.x

Bhan, G., Caldeira, T., Gillespie, K. and Simone, A. (2020) 'The pandemic, Southern urbanisms and collective life'. *Society and Space*, August. Retrieved from: www.societyandspace.org/articles/the-pandemic-southern-urbanisms-and-collective-life

Biswas, S. (2020) 'Coronavirus: India's pandemic lockdown turns into a human tragedy'. BBC News, March 30. Retrieved from: www.bbc.com/news/world-asia-india-52086274

Dahat, P. and Jain, A. (2020) 'Thousands gather at Mumbai's Bandra Station over rumours of train service resumption'. *The Huffington Post*, April 14. Retrieved from: www.huffingtonpost.in/entry/thousands-gather-in-mumbai-over-rumours-of-train-service-resumption_in_5e95db1bc5b606109f60ca4e

Dundoo, S.D. (2020) 'Sonu Sood: "migrant workers built our homes; I couldn't watch them being homeless"'. *The Hindu*, March 27. Retrieved from: www.thehindu.com/entertainment/movies/sonu-sood-migrant-workers-built-our-homes-i-couldnt-watch-them-being-homeless/article31685826.ece

Dutta, A. (2020) 'Survival infrastructures under COVID-19'. Retrieved from: Geography Directions website: https://blog.geographydirections.com/2020/05/13/survival-infrastructures-under-COVID-19/

Edwards, A. (2016) 'UNHCR viewpoint: "refugee" or "migrant" – which is right?' Retrieved from: The UNHCR website: /www. unhcr.org/news/latest/2016/7/55df0e556/unhcr-viewpoint-refugee-migrant-right.html

Gettleman, J. and Schultz, K. (2020) 'Modi Orders 3-Week Total Lockdown for All 1.3 Billion Indians'. *The New York Times*, March 24. Retrieved from: www.nytimes.com/2020/03/24/world/asia/india-coronavirus-lockdown.html

Ghertner, A.D. (2011) 'Gentrifying the state, gentrifying participation: elite governance programs in Delhi'. *International Journal of Urban and Regional Research*, 35(3): 504–32. https://doi.org/10.1111/j.1468-2427.2011.01043.x

Ghertner, A.D. (2015) *Rule by aesthetics: world-class city making in Delhi*. https://doi.org/10.1093/acprof:oso/9780199385560.001.0001

Ghosh, A.K. and Basu Ray Chaudhury, A. (2020) 'Migrant workers and the ethics of care during a pandemic', in R. Samaddar (ed) *Borders of an Epidemic: COVID-19 and Migrant Workers*. Kolkata: Mahanirban Calcutta Research Group, pp 91–7.

Gupta, S., Nair, S., Fernando, B., Varma, V. and Dutta, A. (2020) 'How citizens are helping migrants stranded by the coronavirus lockdown'. *The Indian Express*, May 19. Retrieved from: https://indianexpress.com/article/express-sunday-eye/citizens-helping-migrants-stranded-coronavirus-lockdown-6412617/

March, L. (2020) 'Queer and trans★ geographies of liminality: a literature review'. *Progress in Human Geography*, 20(10): 1–17, https://doi.org/10.1177/0309132520913111

Mishra, D. (2020) 'RTI shows the government did collect data on deaths of migrant workers during lockdown'. *The Wire*, September. Retrieved from: https://thewire.in/rights/centre-indian-railways-lockdown-deaths-migrant-workers-shramik-special-rti

Nath, D. (2020) 'Govt. has no data of migrant workers' death, loss of job'. *The Hindu*, September 14. Retrieved from: www.thehindu.com/news/national/govt-has-no-data-of-migrant-workers-death-loss-of-job/article32600637.ece

Press Trust of India (2020) 'NGOs deserve all appreciation for helping migrants during COVID-19 pandemic: SC'. *The Hindu*, June 9. Retrieved from: www.thehindu.com/news/national/ngos-deserves-all-appreciation-for-helping-migrants-during-COVID-19-pandemic-sc/article31786947.ece

Rao, N. (2013) *House but no garden: apartment living in Bombay's suburbs, 1898–1964*. Retrieved from: www.upress.umn.edu/book-division/books/house-but-no-garden

Roy, A. (2020, April 4) 'The pandemic is a portal'. *Financial Times*. Retrieved from: www.ft.com/content/10d8f5e8-74eb-11ea-95fe-fcd274e920ca

Saxena, C. (2020) 'Experiencing transnational displacement: dwelling, segregation, identity, and host'. *Political Geography*. https://doi.org/10.1016/j.polgeo.2020.102156

Singh, S. (2020) 'Migrant workers crowd Anand Vihar bus terminus to return to their villages'. *The Economic Times*, March 28. Retrieved from: https://economictimes.indiatimes.com/news/politics-and-nation/migrant-workers-crowd-anand-vihar-bus-terminus-to-return-to-their-villages/articleshow/74863940.cms?from=mdr

Singh, S.S. (2020) 'Coronavirus: the mystery of the low COVID-19 numbers in West Bengal'. *The Hindu*, May 1. Retrieved from: www.thehindu.com/news/national/other-states/the-mystery-of-the-low-COVID-19-numbers-in-west-bengal/article31484561.ece

The Wire Analysis (2020) 'Fact check: no, the centre isn't paying for migrant workers' train journeys home'. *The Wire*, May 6. Retrieved from: https://thewire.in/government/indian-railways-migrant-workers-fare

Varma, S. (2020) 'Why India's legal and labour system needs to be reconfigured to really help migrant workers'. *The Wire*, May 19. Retrieved from: https://thewire.in/labour/india-labour-legal-system-migrant-workers

SIXTEEN

Living through a Pandemic in the Shadows of Gentrification and Displacement: Experiences of Marginalized Residents in Waterloo Region, Canada

William Turman, Brian Doucet, and Faryal Diwan

Introduction

What happens to marginalized communities that were already facing gentrification and displacement pressures when a major pandemic arrives? This chapter engages with, listens to and amplifies the experiences of very low-income and unsheltered residents as they deal with the pre-existing conditions of extreme housing challenges and the arrival of the first wave of COVID-19.

This chapter is part of a wider collaboration between the researchers at University of Waterloo (UW) and the Social Development Centre Waterloo Region (SDC), a charitable non-profit, social planning, and community development organization that focuses on advancing social justice and documenting the lived experiences of poverty and homelessness. Throughout the late spring and summer of 2020, we interviewed residents living through both gentrification and the pandemic. In this chapter, we focus on the everyday lives, challenges, experiences, and opportunities of some of the most marginalized members of our community. The pandemic brought new challenges into a landscape that was already hostile to low-income people. Our chapter seeks to amplify their voices and experiences, which is essential for achieving equitable policy outcomes. At the same time, we juxtapose their experiences with some of the dominant narratives of how COVID-19 has impacted the region.

The gentrification context

Our case study is the Region of Waterloo, which is comprised of three contiguous mid-sized cities (Kitchener, Waterloo, and Cambridge) and four rural townships. It ranks among Canada's fastest growing urban areas and has a total population of approximately 620,000. The region is situated 100km west of Toronto, Canada's largest city. Kitchener is the largest of the three cities; like many mid-sized communities, its downtown underwent several decades of decline, beginning in the 1980s. Large old homes were divided up into rooming houses, a cluster of social services organizations emerged, and downtown Kitchener became home to much of the region's very low-income population.

However, over the past decade, a combination of public- and private-investment in the downtown core has led to a remarkable transformation and regeneration, unlike any other mid-sized city in Ontario. Much of this was spurred by the development of a new Light Rail Transit Line, which opened in 2019 and was financed by the Region of Waterloo. Even before a single passenger was carried, more than $3 billion worth of investment was made along the 19km route, much of it in downtown Kitchener. At the same time, downtown was becoming a tech hub; several old factories have been renovated into offices, with Google being the most high-profile occupant. Their officers are in a former rubber factory, and the area surrounding it has been rebranded as the 'Innovation District'.

These developments have placed considerable pressure on low-income communities. Many small apartments have been demolished to make way for new condominium towers, and rooming houses and small apartment buildings have been refurbished in a process known as 'renoviction' – where landlords evict low-income tenants, renovate properties, and then rent them out at higher rates to more affluent households (see Social Development Centre (SDC), 2020). Downtown Kitchener today is a juxtaposition of new condominium towers, trendy restaurants, and placemaking initiatives that exist beside soup kitchens, low-end housing, and a large unsheltered population.

The region was already in a housing crisis before the arrival of COVID-19 (Thompson, 2020a). In this chapter, we examine the housing implications of the pandemic for the region's low-income population. These marginalized voices are largely absent from mainstream planning and policy debates. For this chapter, we draw on 24 interviews with low-income and marginalized residents primarily living within the region's core urban neighborhoods, where gentrification is most evident. Of these interviews, 16 respondents had incomes of less than $25,000, four were seniors, seven lived in social housing, four were unsheltered, four received government supports through disability or unemployment benefits, and five were part of a minority ethnic group. It is also important to note that these categories are fluid and many respondents experienced employment, unemployment, homelessness, and other housing situations within the past five years.

The SDC assists a variety of marginalized residents and communities, including those on low-income, unsheltered, or previously unsheltered individuals, and residents facing eviction. Part of the SDC's role is to advocate for these residents and to amplify their voices within wider planning, policy, and public debates. Because of this long-standing work, the SDC has connections to many community members who could help recruit participants. Interviews were conducted by telephone because face-to-face research was prohibited due to COVID-19 restrictions and because many respondents did not have access to home internet. During the time our interviews were conducted, many businesses and virtually all government buildings (including libraries and community centers) were shut. Our interviews examined two, inter-related issues: longer-term experiences of gentrification and displacement, and how very low-income residents managed during the first wave of the pandemic. Interviews were audio recorded, professionally transcribed, and analyzed by both UW and SDC researchers. Our work and partnership are ongoing, and this chapter presents a snapshot of the impact of COVID-19 on vulnerable populations during the first months of the pandemic.

Living through gentrification

In Kitchener, there is a network of not-for-profits and charities that provide food, shelter, and accessible services and supports. Soup kitchens and regular meals provided by local churches offer not only food, but social spaces to connect with friends and exchange information. In downtown, the owner of a small convenience store, Udanapher (Nadine) Green, assisted many unsheltered individuals by providing access to a warm space, a telephone, washroom, and even credit to buy things in her small store.

For those whose home lives are unhealthy or non-existent, these third spaces are a lifeline. These spaces become the equivalent of living rooms, back yards, and kitchens. In effect, the library, soup kitchen, and even the weekly dinners offered at scattered locations and times across the city are spaces of refuge and home. One retired gentleman living in subsidized housing stated: "I used to go to St John's Kitchen on a regular basis. Not because I needed the food, but there was a whole group of people that I used to connect with there."

Some of the same gentrification and displacement pressures in the housing market were also felt by these non-profits. Some had already been displaced from downtown, such as a foodbank that moved out to the suburbs and a community health center that was replaced by a new courthouse. In 2015, local churches decided to discontinue a winter overnight sheltering program, with the sentiment that the regional government (who is tasked with providing affordable housing and many social services) should not rely on the goodwill of the church community as an expedient solution to chronic homelessness (Record Staff, 2015). Nadine Green was also harassed and her business was evicted in early 2020 (Rubinoff, 2020). In an interview with us, she told us about some of the harassment she faced before she was evicted: "They (the police) are being wicked to me. I would get lots of parking tickets; I got $2,800 worth of parking tickets! Any time I'm in the alleyway, they come give a ticket." There have also been several high-profile examples of renovictions in the downtown core, reducing the supply of affordable housing, especially for those on disability (ODSP) benefits (Thompson, 2019).

Life during the pandemic

On March 17, 2020, the premier of Ontario declared a province-wide state of emergency due to the COVID-19 pandemic, which shut down all non-essential services. The announcement also prohibited gatherings, eat-in dining, and resulted in the closure of facilities such as libraries, schools, community centers, and other public buildings. In practice, this meant that many services and spaces that were necessary for marginalized people closed as well: soup kitchens, non-profits, and charities shut down or dramatically reduced their operations. Public bathrooms in libraries and city hall became inaccessible. Even park and street benches were removed.

Overflow shelters were set up, but they were limited to operating at night and forced people out during the day. Reflecting on these changes, Dan, a resident of several overflow shelters stated:

'To get up at 7:00 in the morning and then they make you leave by 8:00. And so, the thing is, in the middle of the winter and there's no place to go inside, it's all [closed because of] COVID-19 virus. You know, all you could do was go in, get a coffee or something from the window. And there were a few places they had open like the [former] Charles Street [bus] terminal for the washroom, but then that got closed down because of some stupid behavior there. There was the Waterloo Town Square, which I was going to, where you could go into the washroom; but the security would quickly be on you to tell you to get out. So, eventually, it got so cold that you'd have to just ride – you know, the buses were free, which was great. And the LRT. So, we would just get on the bus. And we would ride the bus all day, because we were freezing.'

Stories such as this were common in our interviews. However, they rarely featured in dominant narratives about life during the pandemic. For the middle class, government interventions meant relatively few people lost their homes. The federal government was quick to offer financial relief for those (temporarily) unemployed or without income due to the pandemic, launching the Canada Emergency Response Benefit (CERB). It was a taxable, $2,000 a month benefit for up to four months. However, CERB did not provide assistance to people who were already unemployed, had lost informal employment, or who were on ODSP. It is worth noting that typical ODSP payments, particularly for a single male, are roughly half the amount paid under the CERB. For those without the CERB, the pandemic made life harder for several reasons. For one respondent with diabetes living in affordable, non-profit housing, the small, one-time jobs that allowed them to afford a balanced diet disappeared. For them, "the additional costs that were brought in to play by being in self-quarantine, the lack of work, you know, part time jobs that were available [meant] that I really couldn't afford my rent, it almost cost my leg. Not that my landlord had done anything to increase things, but because I was so close to the edge there was no place to squeeze out anything else".

Challenges related to the lockdown were far greater for those who were already in vulnerable positions. While new telecommuters might have complained about slow internet speeds, the closure of public buildings meant that people without home internet or telephone were entirely cut off from communication and information. Both Nadine, who we introduced earlier, and Bryan, a tradesperson living in a tent in the suburbs, underscored how these various closures created additional challenges for marginalized residents:

'They took up all the benches from downtown. There was no phone to use. And actually, the soup kitchen was closed. The soup kitchen was closed maybe at five, but then Ray of Hope [a shelter] doesn't open until seven. And then between that time there is no place to make a phone call. There is hardly any place for the internet.' (Nadine)

'It's limited the amount of resources that we have out here. You know, like, being able to walk into McDonald's … COVID-19 hit, nobody's allowed in McDonald's. Then it's going to the drive-through, well, people sleeping in a tent, it turns out they don't have a car, so they can't go to the drive-throughs, you know. … simple things, like, you know, walk in McDonald's and buy a drink … buy something for dinner, because you can afford that.' (Bryan)

COVID-19 as a catalyst for positive change

The early phases of the pandemic saw the introduction of several meaningful, though in many cases temporary, measures to support the region's most vulnerable populations. As in other cities (see Kayanan et al, Chapter Seventeen), some of this was bottom-up, community-led. The owner of a small convention space called Lot 42, opened their grounds for people to pitch tents. The space is now called A Better Tent City (ABTC) (see Booth, 2020). Approximately 40 residents set up semi-temporary tiny houses and tents, and the site provides access to bathrooms, a shared kitchen, and communal washing stations. Health services and not-for-profits visit and support the site as part of their scheduled rounds. Nadine Green was active in establishing and supporting the site.

Municipalities have 'assisted' marginalized communities by not enforcing existing bylaws as strictly as they might otherwise do. The city of Kitchener, acknowledging the increased challenges to homeless people, voted to withhold enforcement of zoning bylaw to allow ABTC to continue to operate for one year (Thompson, 2020b). Another publicly visible encampment was permitted to remain for several months through lack of bylaw enforcement. Instead of being evicted on short notice, the landowner, residents, and local government reached an agreement to ensure they had a place to go to after it was shut down.

Another positive development has been the temporary use of hotels to augment space in overcrowded shelters. In March, the House of Friendship, a men's shelter in downtown Kitchener moved some of its residents into the city's Radisson Hotel in order to accommodate social distancing measures (Monteiro, 2020). As Nadine Green noted:

'So the pandemic actually helped the homeless a little more. For some strange reason, it actually helped. Because with the Radisson housing the homeless, you know, a lot of the guys are so happy to get a nice hotel. They're grateful for that. They wouldn't have had that if it wasn't for the pandemic. If it wasn't for the pandemic, I wouldn't be at LOT42 because that would be a venue for people with money, and they would never have let any homeless people even be there. The pandemic switched things around, I believe.'

The challenge will be to turn these temporary measures into long-term, transformative ones (see Parsell et al, 2020).

COVID-19 as a threat

However, there are still many pressing issues facing marginalized residents, particularly with respect to housing. The question also remains to what extent the measures implemented in 2020 will prove to only be temporary? Housing has become one of the biggest challenges, and therefore political issues, in Waterloo Region in recent years. The summer of 2020 saw one of the hottest local property markets on record, not only because of pent-up demand, but because the Region of Waterloo provides an affordable alternative to nearby Toronto (Davis, 2020). This trend of leaving the Toronto region in search of more affordable housing in nearby cities such as Kitchener has been evident for many years; early indications show that these migration patterns have accelerated during the pandemic (van der Merwe and Doucet, 2021).

While the provincial government halted evictions in March 2020, this was a temporary measure, and even during the ban, there were many reports of harassment of tenants by threatening them with evictions (Press Progress, 2020). By July 2020, the Ontario Landlord and Tenant Board received more than 6,000 applications to evict tenants for not paying their rent during the pandemic. Reflecting on the wider housing situation, Katherine, a 61-year-old ODSP recipient, noted:

'A lot of people are going to be displaced because there's not going to be anywhere for them to live, because people are going to be selling and then there's going to be these greedy people that are going to be buying the houses. And there's going to be more ghost houses. So I think that the homelessness is going to increase and the shortage of housing is going to increase. The rich are going to get richer and the poor are going to get poorer.'

In July 2020, the Province of Ontario passed Bill 184, colloquially known as the 'eviction bill' because it makes it easier for landlords to evict tenants. Many non-profits and charities that provide housing are also under threat because many of their programs have been put on hold. As a result, housing remains a precarious issue for many low-income residents.

It is important to stress that much of the gentrification and displacement literature focuses not only on housing, but on the loss of one's connection to community, or sense of belonging as well (Shaw and Hagemans, 2015; Kern, 2016). Our research demonstrates how the pandemic has accelerated many forms of displacement from the region's urban core. While the closure of streets to automobiles to make way for outdoor dining and pedestrian spaces have been praised as creating hip spaces for business and consumption, these spaces exclude those on very low incomes. There is an irony that while many public benches were being removed as a way of deterring unsheltered populations from gathering in groups, private restaurants opened up outdoor dining facilities on public streets and sidewalks (Yasin and Ferguson, 2021; see also March and Lehrer, Volume 3; De Backer and Melgaço, Volume 3).

Conclusion

For our very low-income respondents, the COVID-19 pandemic is having an extreme impact on everyday life, with an outsized impact on those with little or no housing (see also Xavier, Chapter Seven; Parker and de Kadt, Chapter Eleven; Banerjee and Das, Chapter Fifteen; Beeckmans and Oosterlyck, Volume 3). Three points are worth reflecting on if we are to see transformative change.

First, our understanding of the experiences of gentrification needs to continue to evolve beyond purely thinking about experiences of housing; the pandemic has led to the abrupt loss of important third spaces that are about both physical displacement (the closure of a shelter) as well as psychological or phenomenological displacement, which is becoming increasingly important in the literature on experiencing gentrification (Shaw and Hagemans, 2015; Kern, 2016; Elliott-Cooper et al, 2019). Even for low-income residents who have apartments further away from downtown, these downtown spaces function as their 'living room', and these changes represent what Shaw and Hagemans (2015) refer to as 'loss of place' and Kern (2016) calls 'slow violence'. This displacement was both a pre-existing condition before the pandemic and has been accelerated because of it.

Second, while challenges for low-income residents have grown because of the pandemic, there are some bright spots. Businesses, not-for-profits, and local governments have given money, space, and resources to deal with the immediate crisis, particularly for the most marginalized. The challenge is how to turn these temporary measures into transformative changes that address the causes of poverty and homelessness, rather than dealing with its consequences (which have been amplified in the age of COVID-19).

One of the ways to do this relates to our final point: that inclusive and equitable change can only come about when the lived experiences of marginalized populations are fully incorporated into the planning, policy and political decision-making as to how to respond to the pandemic. This means giving those with lived experience of poverty meaningful positions at decision-making tables. Only then can we begin to redress the injustices brought about by gentrification, evictions, and displacement on the most vulnerable members of society.

References

Booth, L. (2020) 'Residents move from tents into cabins at Kitchener's newest settlement for the homeless'. *Waterloo Region Record*, June 14.

Davis, B. (2020) 'Dozens of bids, offers $100,000 over asking define an "absolutely wild" real estate market'. *Waterloo Region Record*, September 3.

Elliott-Cooper, A., Hubbard, P. and Lees, L. (2019) 'Moving beyond Marcuse: gentrification, displacement and the violence of un-homing'. *Progress in Human Geography*, 44(3): 492–509, https://doi.org/10.1177/0309132519830511

Kern, L. (2016) 'Rhythms of gentrification: eventfulness and slow violence in a happening neighbourhood'. *Cultural Geographies*, 23(3): 441–57, https://doi.org/10.1177/1474474015591489

Monteiro, L. (2020) 'House of Friendship moves to Radisson Hotel'. *Waterloo Region Record*, March 24.

Parsell, C., Clarke, A. and Kuskoff, E. (2020) 'Understanding responses to homelessness during COVID-19: an examination of Australia'. *Housing Studies*, 1–14, https://doi.org/10.1080/02673037.2020.1829564

Record Staff (2015) 'Closed: last out of the cold homeless shelter ends overnight stays in Waterloo'. *Waterloo Chronicle*, June 25.

Rubinoff, J. (2020) ' "I'm not going anywhere!" says Nadine Green, Kitchener's champion of the underdog'. *Waterloo Region Record*, February 7.

Shaw, K.S. and Hagemans, I.W. (2015) ' "Gentrification without displacement" and the consequent loss of place: the effects of class transition on low-income residents of secure housing in gentrifying areas'. *International Journal of Urban and Regional Research*, 39(2): 323–41.

Social Development Centre (SDC) (2020) *Life Stories of Displacement*, www.waterlooregion.org/life-stories-of-displacement

Thompson, C. (2019) 'Caught up in the rapid changes transforming Kitchener's core: evicted tenants struggling to find new homes as low-cost apartments undergo renovations'. *Waterloo Region Record*, 16 April.

Thompson, C. (2020a) 'New report details growing housing crisis in Kitchener'. *Waterloo Region Record*, January 6.

Thompson, C. (2020b) 'Kitchener to allow Tent City site to stay for up to a year'. *Waterloo Region Record*, July 6.

van der Merwe, J. and Doucet, B. (2021) 'Housing challenges, mid-sized cities and the COVID-19 pandemic: critical reflections from Waterloo Region'. *Canadian Planning and Policy*, 2021(1): 70–90.

Yasin, A. and Ferguson, D. (2021) 'Pandemic patios and "flat white" urbanism'. *Plan Canada*, 60(4): 21–6.

SEVENTEEN

Cities Under Lockdown: Public Health, Urban Vulnerabilities, and Neighborhood Planning in Dublin

Carla Maria Kayanan, Niamh Moore-Cherry, and Alma Clavin

'All the bloody student accommodation in Dublin 8, I don't think they have one park, you know, they haven't given back, they've put up all these buildings but they haven't given back to the community in terms of space.' (Social Service provider for Fatima Groups United, personal interview, July 9, 2020)

Introduction

Since its initial appearance in Wuhan, China, in late 2019, much attention has focused on the disproportionate spread and impact of COVID-19 in metropolitan areas and on patterns and rates of infection and morbidity in cities, neighborhoods, and across different ethnic backgrounds (Hamidi et al, 2020; Mills et al, 2020). Across the globe, a key strategy to contain and mitigate the worst effects of the virus has been through halting or limiting mobility through 'lockdowns'. #Staysafe

#stayhome public health messaging appeared across print, social, and broadcast media in many countries. Given the short timeframes to assess impact, less attention has been paid in the academic literature to date on the differential impacts of public health restrictions to contain the virus on particular groups, individuals, and communities. While it is still too early to fully document what the long-term consequences might be, in this chapter we detail the immediate impacts of 'lockdown' through the experience of one community – Dublin 8, an inner-city neighborhood in southwest Dublin. We argue that the experience of 'lockdown' is contextually dependent and, through interviews with key community workers, social care providers, and residents, elucidate how already-disadvantaged communities were disproportionately impacted, compounding their vulnerabilities.

Over the past 30 years, Dublin (Ireland) has experienced extensive urban regeneration through 'flagship' commercial projects but also through social housing estate regeneration programs, many controversially initiated under public-private partnerships. Success has been limited, with developments critiqued for failing to address the specific needs of targeted communities and the city's general housing accessibility and affordability crises (Hearne, 2011). The longer-term implications of this neglect and policy failure became acutely evident during COVID-19 mobility restrictions, particularly in relation to access to green and other forms of safe outdoor spaces.

Dublin 8 is characterized by significant institutional land, at least three large-scale social housing schemes that have been the subject of 'regeneration', railway lands and 19th-century housing built for former railway workers currently undergoing gentrification. Historically a lower-income neighborhood, repeated intervention by a range of government, construction, and real estate growth interests over three decades, has triggered concerns over a 'Docklands-style makeover' (Thomas, 2019), a reference to Dublin's newest unaffordable and inward-looking tech-neighborhood. Budding start-ups, high-end student accommodation, hotel construction, and rising rents point to the 'upgrading' of Dublin 8, but social, economic, and health inequalities are now more pronounced. The community's experience during lockdown demonstrates the need to reconceptualize the idea of 'home' and return urban planning to its public health roots to deliver more just and healthy cities.

Living with lockdown

On February 29, 2020, the media reported the first positive COVID-19 case in Ireland. The government's first response, containing the virus, followed World Health Organization (WHO) and European Centre for Disease Control (ECDC) guidelines. By early March, the government moved into phase 2 'delay' by closing schools and other educational and cultural institutions for an initial two-week period. On March 27, the government placed the country on full 'lockdown' with people restricted in their movement to a 2km radius of their place of residence, extended to 5km on May 5. Geographic limitations were lifted gradually from county to national-level, although 'local lockdowns' have occurred.

The stay-at-home order pre-supposed a safe and adequate home environment for all. Immediate concerns emerged around homeless people and the need to secure emergency accommodation rapidly. Those with less visible challenging home and housing situations received scant attention. In Dublin 8, for example, a large proportion of the most vulnerable groups live in social housing estates, some suffering years of neglect. In January 2017, Dublin City Council reported that 2,132 households were on the housing waiting list for Dublin 8, with 184 households having waited over ten years. Dolphin House, a large social housing complex finally undergoing regeneration, has few units with balconies. Outdoor space, where available, is poorly maintained and perceived as unsafe.

'Most of the community at Dolphin House, they live in 1950s housing blocks without their own private external garden or balcony. It's really difficult for the children to access somewhere safe to play and that had a real issue on families.' (Social service provider for Dolphin House, personal interview, July 10, 2020).

Nearby, St. Michael's estate (12.1 acres), is undergoing a long-awaited process of redevelopment. Residents are concerned that both the housing and wider needs of the community will continue to be ignored. While the site has a potential of 420 new units, only 123 (30 percent) will be social housing units with 55 of these reserved for sheltered housing for the elderly. Though the remaining units (70 percent) will be cost-rental as opposed to market rents, the pressures that these communities are under to maintain a home in the city is acute. Fatima, the third large-scale social housing estate, underwent regeneration and substantial privatization in the early 2000s. Though it does not face the same neglected living conditions, it does share problems with regard to green space access.

Rather than using available land to enhance the public realm and address identified community infrastructure gaps, in the past decade, private development has favored student accommodation and hotels. As stated by a community development worker: "More land disappears that could have been greened, I guess, or that could have been made available for social housing" (personal interview, July 7, 2020). The twinning of housing and greening in this sentiment is critical: green space and the wider urban environment is often sacrificed to maximize real estate development. The wider implications of this brick-and-mortar approach to development, rather than sensitive placemaking, are well appreciated within the local community. These were brought into sharp focus during the height of the lockdown when local neighborhoods (within 2km) became central to individual and community resilience. As scholars have long argued – and the pandemic has certainly

Figure 17.1: Social housing estates and green space within a 400m radius

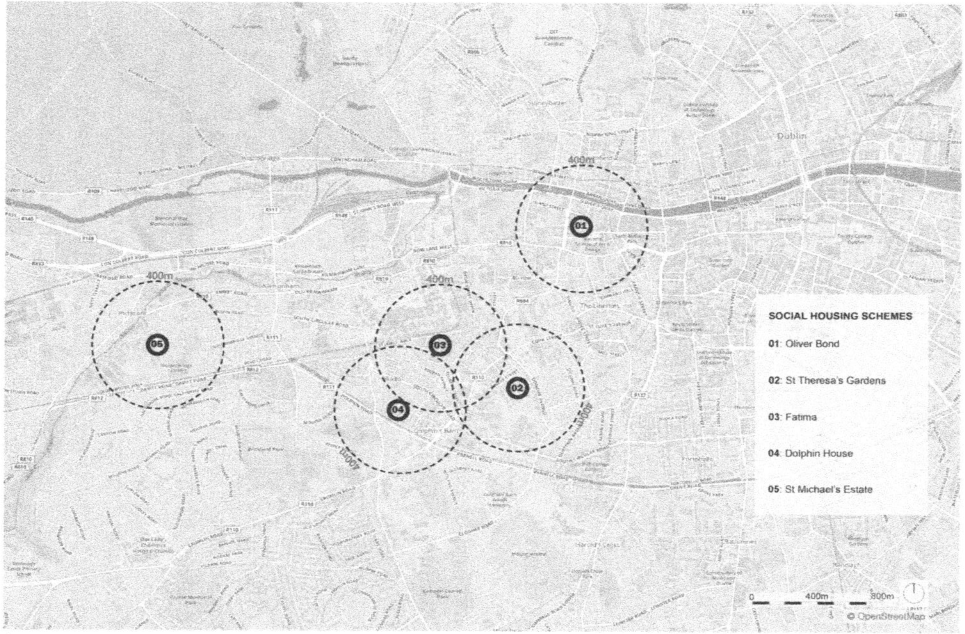
SOCIAL HOUSING SCHEMES
01: Oliver Bond
02: St Theresa's Gardens
03: Fatima
04: Dolphin House
05: St Michael's Estate
400m
Dublin
0
400m
800m
© OpenStreetMap

Source: map created by author

emphasized – access to green space is vital for public health, mental health, and overall well-being (Callaghan et al, 2020). Furthermore, it is the 'closest-in' greenspace, within 300 meters of home, that directly impacts mental well-being (Houlden et al, 2019), with 400m and 800m radius representing a five-minute and 10/15-minute walk respectively (see Figure 17.1).

Youth, families, and community bonds

One of the benefits of repeated government interventions and more recent regeneration initiatives in the area has been the hiring of youth workers to the estates and neighborhood. As of the most recently available Irish Census (2016), 31 percent of the population of the electoral area comprising Dolphin House and Fatima is under the age of 24, with 16 percent of families comprising single mothers. Youth workers expressed concerns over the effect of the pandemic on them. When lockdown was imposed, social workers moved quickly to shift their resources online. However, youth workers and community members demonstrated digital poverty from the lack of infrastructure and equipment, as well as from the absence of technical knowledge and online etiquette. Forty-one percent of households in this area have no personal computer in the home with 28 percent having no internet access (Irish Census, 2016).

The closure of schools, youth clubs, and community centers disproportionately impacted young people. Without space and the ability to meet physically, social workers struggled to keep young adults engaged. Though some tried FIFA and Fortnite videogames to maintain lines of communication with trust-worthy adults (Freyne, 2020), disengaged youths took to the streets, often in large groups, flagrantly disregarding lockdown and physical distancing measures. As one respondent stated, "At one point we met 40 young people hanging out in a group" (personal interview, July 22, 2020). The poor-quality environment available to these young people is summed up by one youth worker:

'At the back of Tyrone place [adjacent to St. Michael's estate] there is green space and a playground, but they are not in the best of condition. We were using it for a family fun day, and it was filthy dirty. There are green spots at the back of the flats, but they are not in a state to be used properly. There is a balance between people not using and respecting it and not being good enough to be respected.' (Personal interview, July 22, 2020)

As high-quality living environments are built into privatized apartment blocks, basic public community infrastructure becomes disinvested. And while the state provides initial capital funding for infrastructure under the umbrella of 'social regeneration', long-term commitment is lacking:

'The community center has an Astro turf pitch on the back of it … They never managed that space. Initially it was part of the community center. There are two pitches on that and that's a wasted space. It's not maintained, it's not taken care of. For us, we would love a space like that for young people. It would be constantly used. We wanted to use it for our street games, but it was unusable.' (Youth worker, personal interview, July 22, 2020)

The absence of appropriate outdoor spaces, coupled with the closure of community services during lockdown, demonstrated the extent to which vulnerable communities are 'living on the edge' and the deep inequities across and within neighborhoods. Whereas communities in more affluent parts of the city had access to regional and local parks, as well as high-quality and safe local green spaces, under the #stayhome public health order, large groups of young people in Dublin 8 competed for the few spaces available for young families, with proximate access to Dublin's largest destination park (Phoenix Park) fragmented by busy roads and transport infrastructure. Parents and younger children struggled to maintain physical distancing from groups of youth and, in some cases, retreated indoors.

However, lockdown also foregrounded the strong sense of solidarity that exists within Dublin 8. Solidarity has been a key feature of the pandemic response globally but often discussed at a more abstract, macro level. In communities where the withdrawal of community and public services as a result of lockdown created a void, existing community bonds became critical to resilience. One social care provider interviewed explained how, throughout lockdown, the community worked together to visit and look after isolated individuals, organize food drives, and maintain social bonds. Another respondent commented on the tight-knit networks that enabled the organization to extend its reach during the hardest times. The power of social bonds to provide support and alleviate the worst social impacts of a pandemic are clear, further justifying the need for community and social infrastructure planning to complement market-based forms of development. Planning for a post-COVID-19 world must recognize not just the challenges but also the learnings from real-world experiences of life under lockdown.

Conclusion

Historically, actors and institutions in charge of designing and managing cities have introduced measures, rules, and regulations to ensure the health and well-being of residents. The increased neoliberalization and financialization of the city have shifted planning from its origins in public health and redistribution to a growth-first, materialist logic (see Wilson, Volume 3). COVID-19 and the differential experiences of public health measures within urban settings have thrown into sharp focus entrenched inequalities and issues of social justice. Already-vulnerable communities were disproportionately impacted by stay-at-home orders that relied on normative understandings of home (as a safe, comfortable environment) and the availability of high-quality amenity spaces to sustain mental health and well-being (see also Warnock, Chapter Twelve). Issues of density are also critical in terms of the nature of housing and the wider environment. Residential overcrowding, being able to access adequate internal space, and the ability to self-isolate safely are prescient planning concerns (see Hubbard, Chapter Four). Maximizing profit from particular parcels of land through minimal space standards is now a significant public health hazard. Assuring local access to green spaces within neighborhoods for exercise and respite from the solitude and mobility-constraints of a lockdown need to become standard aspects of forward planning (Dobson; Whitten and Massini; Rodrigues et al, all Volume 3).

While we are only starting to understand the way that COVID-19 and public health restrictions have impacted urban residents, what we know so far highlights the complex relationships between individualism and solidarity, between social care services and community welfare. Reflecting on this is an important part of charting, understanding, and learning from recent urban experiences. The illustrative case study of Dublin 8 also highlights the complexity of asserting claims to urban space and the right to use it, in a context where open, quality, amenity space is a precious commodity. The global pandemic and recent experiences have thrown into sharp relief that home has become much more than just shelter – access to affordable and adequate individual dwelling places has a wider significance for the wider urban community.

Note

The authors would like to acknowledge the Irish Research Council's Coalesce and New Foundation strands, as well as the EPA Research Program 2014–20 for their support with this work.

References

Callaghan, A., McCombe, G., Harrold, A., McMeel, C., Mills, G., Moore-Cherry, N. and Cullen, W. (2020) 'The impact of green spaces on mental health in urban settings: a scoping review'. *Journal of Mental Health*, https://doi.org/10.1080/09638237.2020.1755027

Freyne, P. (2020) 'Fortnite is keeping teenagers from falling through the cracks'. *Irish Times*, May 30.

Hamidi, S., Sabouri, S. and Ewing, R. (2020) 'Does density aggravate the COVID-19 pandemic? Early findings and lessons for planners'. *Journal of the American Planning Association*, 86(4): 495–509.

Hearne, R. (2011) *Public Private Partnerships in Ireland: Failed Experiment or the Way Forward for the State?* (1st edn). Manchester: Manchester University Press.

Houlden, V., Porto de Albuquerque, J., Weich, S. and Jarvis, S. (2019) 'A spatial analysis of proximate greenspace and mental wellbeing in London'. *Applied Geography*, 109: 102036, https://doi.org/10.1016/j.apgeog.2019.102036

Irish Census (2016) Retrieved from: www.cso.ie

Mills, G., Cullen, W., Moore-Cherry, N. and Foley, R. (2020) 'Making sense of publicly available data on COVID-19 in Ireland', https://doi.org/10.1101/2020.05.13.20101089

Thomas, C. (2019) 'Concerns of over-development in Dublin 8 as "Docklands- style makeover" proposed'. *The Journal*, August 31. Retrieved from: https://jrnl.ie/4787198

EIGHTEEN

Conclusion

Brian Doucet, Pierre Filion, and Rianne van Melik

The home is one of the key arenas in which the COVID-19 pandemic has been both fought and experienced. 'Staying at home' has been one of the main public health measures used to combat the spread of the virus. However, the ability to follow these guidelines varies tremendously due to both pre-existing inequalities and those that have either been introduced, or amplified because of the pandemic. While housing is central to this volume, it is becoming increasingly clear that discussions regarding housing, land use, urban form, economic development, transportation, and inequality that have long been treated as separate conversations need to be part of the same planning and policy debates. This was evident before the arrival of the COVID-19 pandemic, but the need to think across disciplines and themes is more urgent now than ever. The chapters in this volume examine how varied housing issues intersect with work, proximity, ability, class, design, discrimination, and racism to magnify challenges; likewise, chapters in other volumes also discuss housing in reference to communities, public space and planning.

Living in overcrowded housing is strongly correlated to precarious, insecure, or insufficient employment income. Racism and racial discrimination limit the housing opportunities of many people. Many low-income residents in cities around the world have no choice but to reside in (socially and/or spatially) peripheral neighborhoods far from employment opportunities because that is all they can afford. These intersections produce a context where the virus can thrive, but also shapes our variegated experiences with urban life during the pandemic (McKee et al, 2020; Patel et al, 2020).

Volume 2 has shown that there is little new about urban inequities as a result of the COVID-19 pandemic. Thinking holistically across the urban world, the pandemic has done two things. First, it has amplified and magnified existing economic, social, spatial, and racial inequalities, particularly when it comes to housing. Wescley Xavier (Chapter Seven) summed it up best with his subtitle about housing in Brazil: 'poor people, victims again'. That does not mean that this is simply the same old story; as Rogers and Power (2020) note, some aspects of housing policy shifted extremely rapidly in the face of unprecedented challenges. Around the world, homeless populations have been provided with accommodation and shelter (see Turman et al, Chapter Sixteen). However, much of what we have seen thus far during the pandemic has been designed to be temporary (see Parsell et al, 2020). Vilenica et al (2020) question who these measures are designed to prop up: vulnerable populations, or a capitalist system that relies on extracting wealth from housing? In spite, or perhaps because of this, the general trend during the first phases of the pandemic was of the continued acceleration of social, spatial, and racial inequalities. As both Tunstall and Hubbard (Chapter Two and Chapter Four, respectively) note, housing systems were broken before COVID-19 arrived, and the pandemic has made housing conditions, experiences, and opportunities far worse for many. To date, we have seen little evidence that these trends are reversing. While we have not been able to cover all aspects of housing during the pandemic, such as increases in domestic violence and the dilution of the home as a private space (since everyone can see our kitchens on a Zoom call), it is clear that of the trends we have covered, pre-existing inequalities have been magnified.

The second thing that the pandemic has done has been to tear back the curtain on many of these pre-existing inequalities. While the public, politicians, and policy makers may look on with horror at the news of deaths in long-term care homes, evictions during the height of the pandemic, or overcrowding that is now in the spotlight, for urban researchers or advocates who have studied these topics, there is little unsurprising news. That many of these inequities and injustices are now on full display perversely gives some glimmer of hope, that they will climb up the political priority list and that meaningful and transformational ideas may be more receptive now that these issues are in plain sight. It is worth stressing that many of the solutions that scholars and advocates have been calling for for many years – new social housing, banning unjust evictions, rent controls, and curbing property speculation – are just as relevant in the age of COVID-19 as they were before. Addressing housing challenges in a time of global pandemic is less about devising new ideas and more about implementing what have long been seen as solutions to unequal and unjust cities.

Of course, there is little 'new' knowledge about these conditions for those who live through them. While living in overcrowded, unsafe, or insecure housing has made life tougher during the pandemic – in economic, social, and health terms – these experiences rarely make it onto the front page of the newspaper, or into planning and policy reports. While specific experiences vary from place to place, one common theme that this book highlights is that those whose lives are most impacted by unequal and unjust housing systems tend to have the least powerful voice in making and shaping those systems. Planning and policy debates tend not to incorporate lived experiences of poverty, or housing precarity into the decision-making rooms.

This was true before the arrival of COVID-19, but it takes on a greater sense of urgency as inequalities grow, and a 'K'-shaped recovery is emerging as a dominant trend in housing, and the wider economies. Too often, however, urban policy is dominated by addressing concerns at the top end of the 'K' rather than the bottom.

While issues of housing have rocketed up the political priority ladder in many cities and countries during the pandemic, there is a danger that the planning and policy solutions to address these challenges will be aimed squarely at middle-class segments of society. This might look like policies to open up new land for the development of larger homes on the urban periphery, in order to meet a growing demand for larger houses with home offices, particularly for those looking to leave smaller apartments and condominiums in city centers. However, solutions such as this will do little to alleviate the plight of the most vulnerable urban residents, who have struggled to obtain safe, secure, and affordable housing for decades.

There is no shortage of potential urban futures. But instead of asking what cities of the future will look like, contributors to this series of books have examined what conditions need to change in order to create more equitable and just urban futures. This has been done through careful analysis and reflection of the context that produces unequal cities, both before the pandemic and during it. This knowledge is necessary in order to influence the planning and policy decisions that will ultimately shape post-pandemic cities.

Our global collection of chapters highlights a common theme throughout the world: marginalized communities lack the ability to assert their voices at the decision-making table. While the curtain has been pulled back on many urban inequalities, this has not yet transitioned into these experiences and voices being central to how we respond to the pandemic. Despite increased mainstream attention towards urban inequalities in the wake of COVID-19, the voices of those with lived experiences of poverty, injustice, or marginalization are still largely invisible in mainstream planning and policy debates. One of the key purposes of this volume – and this entire series – has been to acknowledge, assemble, and amplify these voices in order that they play a much more central and decisive role in shaping urban responses to the pandemic. We have sought to turn up the volume on these lived experiences in the hope that they cannot be ignored. This is, however, only a first step that must ultimately progress towards shifting power relations in planning and policymaking.

Therefore, the key challenge moving forward is how to meaningfully include those with lived experiences of poverty, overcrowding, and substandard or inadequate housing, or those who face discrimination in the housing market, at the center of the decision-making table. With so many urban futures possible, who is present at those tables, who is not, what roles they play, and what power they have will be central to shaping the future of cities and whether or not they will become more equitable places. As the COVID-19 pandemic accelerates the pre-existing inequalities in our cities and societies, it is becoming increasingly clear a just, equitable, and transformative recovery from this pandemic can only come about if these voices are listened to and their lived experiences turned into meaningful policies that directly address the root causes of housing inequity and injustice.

References

McKee, K., Pearce, A. and Leahy, S. (2020) 'The unequal impact of COVID-19 on black, Asian, minority ethnic and refugee communities'. *UK Collaborative Centre for Housing Research*, May 6, https://housingevidence.ac.uk/the-unequal-impact-of-COVID-19-on-black-asian-minority-ethnic-and-refugee-communities/

Parsell, C., Clarke, A. and Kuskoff, E. (2020) 'Understanding responses to homelessness during COVID-19: an examination of Australia'. *Housing Studies*, 1–14, https://doi.org/10.1080/02673037.2020.1829564

Patel, J.A., Nielsen, F.B.H., Badiani, A.A., Assi, S., Unadkat, V.A., Patel, B., Ravindrane, R. and Wardle, H. (2020) 'Poverty, inequality and COVID-19: the forgotten vulnerable'. *Public Health*, 183: 110–11.

Rogers, D. and Power, E. (2020) 'Housing policy and the COVID-19 pandemic: the importance of housing research during this health emergency'. *International Journal of Housing Policy*, 20(2): 177–83.

Vilenica, A., McElroy, E., Ferreri, M., Fernández Arrigoitia, M., García-Lamarca, M. and Lancione, M. (2020) 'COVID-19 and housing struggles: the (re) makings of austerity, disaster capitalism, and the no return to normal'. *Radical Housing Journal*, 2(1): 9–28.

Index

References to endnotes show both the page number and the note number (for example, 231n3).

Lightning Source UK Ltd.
Milton Keynes UK
UKHW022151120722
405758UK00005B/315